Fifty Is the New Fifty

Also by Suzanne Braun Levine

Inventing the Rest of Our Lives: Women in Second Adulthood

Father Courage: What Happens When Men Put Family First

Bella Abzug: How One Tough Broad from the Bronx Fought Jim Crow and Joe McCarthy, Pissed Off Jimmy Carter, Battled for the Rights of Women and Workers, Rallied Against War and for the Planet, and Shook Up Politics Along the Way, an oral history (with Mary Thom)

Fifty Is the New Fifty

Ten Life Lessons for
Women in Second Adulthood

Suzanne Braun Levine

Viking

VIKING
Published by the Penguin Group
Penguin Group (USA) Inc., 375 Hudson Street, New York, New York 10014, U.S.A.
Penguin Group (Canada), 90 Eglinton Avenue East, Suite 700, Toronto, Ontario,
Canada M4P 2Y3 (a division of Pearson Penguin Canada Inc.)
Penguin Books Ltd, 80 Strand, London WC2R 0RL, England
Penguin Ireland, 25 St. Stephen's Green, Dublin 2, Ireland (a division of Penguin Books Ltd)
Penguin Books Australia Ltd, 250 Camberwell Road, Camberwell, Victoria 3124, Australia
(a division of Pearson Australia Group Pty Ltd)
Penguin Books India Pvt Ltd, 11 Community Centre, Panchsheel Park,
New Delhi – 110 017, India
Penguin Group (NZ), 67 Apollo Drive, Rosedale, North Shore 0632, New Zealand
(a division of Pearson New Zealand Ltd)
Penguin Books (South Africa) (Pty) Ltd, 24 Sturdee Avenue, Rosebank,
Johannesburg 2196, South Africa

Penguin Books Ltd, Registered Offices: 80 Strand, London WC2R 0RL, England

First published in 2009 by Viking Penguin, a member of Penguin Group (USA) Inc.

10 9 8 7 6 5 4 3 2 1

Excerpt from "The New Old Woman" by Robin Morgan (from the forthcoming collection *Dark Matter: New Poems* by Robin Morgan). Copyright © 2007 by Robin Morgan. Reprinted by permission of the author.

While the author has made every effort to provide accurate telephone numbers and Internet addresses at the time of publication, neither the publisher nor the author assumes any responsibility for errors, or for changes that occur after publication. Further, publisher does not have any control over and does not assume any responsibility for author or third-party Web sites or their content.

LIBRARY OF CONGRESS CATALOGING IN PUBLICATION DATA
Levine, Suzanne.
Fifty is the new fifty : ten life lessons for women in second adulthood / Suzanne Braun Levine.
p.   cm.
Includes bibliographical references and index.
ISBN 978-0-670-02068-3
  1. Middle age—Psychological aspects.   I. Title.
HQ1059.4.L48 2009
155.6'6—dc22   2008027445

Printed in the United States of America

For Bob

Acknowledgments

With tremendous gratitude to my at-home editor and husband, Bob Levine, and my truly masterful in-house editor, Wendy Wolf, I also want to thank the editors of *More* magazine for helping me shape my ideas about Second Adulthood. Thanks also to my agent, Janis Donnaud. I am grateful for the invaluable tech support I got from Reed Berkowitz, Karen Grenke, Rose Heredia, and my beloved son, Josh, "Mr. Fix-it." Then there is the other and very precious kind of support: the love and encouragement of my indispensable "circle of trust." And with this book there is a new source of information and goodwill: the 350 women who have signed up to be online "friends of Second Adulthood" and share their own experiences with me, and now with you, the readers. My mother, Esther Bernson Braun, remains an inspiration, and my dear daughter, Joanna, already embodies the energy, independence, and effectiveness that I still aspire to. Thank you all!

Contents

Acknowledgments   *vii*

Lesson One   Fifty Is the New Fifty   1

Lesson Two   Nothing Changes if Nothing Changes   22

Lesson Three   *No* Is Not a Four-Letter Word   42

Lesson Four   A "Circle of Trust" Is a Must   63

Lesson Five   Every Crisis Creates a "New Normal"   85

Lesson Six   Do Unto Yourself as You Have Been
Doing Unto Others   104

Lesson Seven   Age Is Not a Disease   125

Lesson Eight   Your Marriage *Can* Make It   145

Lesson Nine   You *Do* Know What You Want
to Do with the Rest of Your Life   160

Lesson Ten   *Both* Is the New *Either/Or*   180

Bibliography   *191*

Web Sites and Organizations   *195*

Index   *207*

Lesson One

Fifty Is the New Fifty

We could not act our age if we did not know our age. . . . We live in the biochemistry of our bodies, and not in years; we live in the interaction between that biochemistry and its greatest product—the human mind—and not in a series of decades marked by periodic lurches of change.

—Dr. Sherwin B. Nuland, *The Art of Aging: A Doctor's Prescription for Well-being*

Fifty is the new fifty. Sixty, I hasten to add, is also the new sixty, and seventy the new seventy. And the women who are the new fifty, sixty, and seventy wouldn't want to be anything else. Some people think they get the reinvention process we are going through when they extrapolate down a decade or two—"I see," they say encouragingly, "Fifty is the new thirty!" as if the reward of what is clearly a major shift in outlook is a new lease on youth. That is not it at all. I have discovered that most women in Second Adulthood are very happy being where they are—they don't want to go back to any of their earlier stages or decades. And while we would all like to be stronger and fresher—and more admired (or at least respected) by the world we live in—few of us would like to be literally younger. "The great thing about getting older," magical writer Madeleine L'Engle, who lived well into her nineties, said, "is that you don't lose all the other ages you've been." We are at a point where our lives are finally beginning to add up.

The assumption is that youth—or at least younger—is the ideal state and that given a choice, no woman in her right mind would relinquish it. I have found the opposite to be true. Many of us are delighting in rejecting that backward-looking mind-set and focusing on (to paraphrase the song from *The King and I*) "the beautiful and new things I am learning about *me* day by day." The range of things to learn about ourselves is now as wide as it hasn't been since we were adolescents. So much about our bodies, our thinking, our relationships, our approach to the world is under review—by us, for a change. And the more we revise, the more we uncover new aspects of ourselves in the process, and the more we discover that we are not who we were when we were younger.

The challenge of this stage of life is not to "get over getting older," as some suggest, but to get to know ourselves in this new context. Who is this person who hears herself say "I don't care what other people think anymore" and loves the sound of it? Who is giving up high heels or belts simply because they are uncomfortable? Who is questioning the nature of her relationships and the meaning of her work? Who is ready to try some new and totally out-of-character experiences on for size? Who knows that life and death is no metaphor, but forges on?

Older is almost irrelevant to these questions—except for the last one. Yet to listen to the society we live in, you would think that you have to stay young—and look young—to be happy. And we buy (literally) into that message, spending millions on age-defying cosmetics, surgery, drugs, and making a book that promises to teach us *How Not to Look Old* a best seller. Even Gloria Steinem, who made such a point of acknowledging her *age* ("This is what forty looks like!" and fifty, sixty, and now seventy), admitted that she had some trouble dealing with *aging*. "Though I would have decried all the actresses, athletes, and other worshipers of youth who were unable to imagine a changed future—a few of whom have even chosen death *over* aging"—she wrote in *Revolution from Within,* "I had been falling into the same trap." An encounter with breast cancer—and her mortality—helped her confront her "denial and defiance" and begin to listen to and adapt her life to her body as it was changing. One unexpected reward for this revised worldview was that she, who had always been considered a great beauty, began to feel liberated from the "epithet of 'the pretty one.'" "If that sounds odd," she explains, "think about working as hard as you can and then discovering that whatever you accomplish is attributed to your looks."

Acclaimed actress Helen Mirren, who is sixty-two, has expressed a similar sentiment. "Being a sexual object is mortifying and irritating, yet it's giving you power—an awful power that you've done nothing to deserve, a powerless power," she told *More* magazine. "I think some young women fall in love with that power, and it's really objectifying. And when it starts falling away, it's an incredible relief." As for chronological age, she had this to say: "When you're 16, you think 28 is so old! And then you get to 28 and it's fabulous. You think, then, what about 42? Ugh! And then 42 is great. As you reach each age, you gain the understanding and experience you need to deal with it and enjoy it."

Our internalized ageism creates an unnecessary but clear and present danger to making the most of this exhilarating moment in our lives. We are moving ahead, but not in the way that the actuaries and youth marketers think. Understanding that *you are not who you were, only older* frees up the imagination and mobilizes one's resources to manage adversity and seize upon serendipity. From this perspective, change is not an enemy but a potential, a force that can be harnessed to shed old identities and embrace new ones, a process that over time creates as many opportunities as it forecloses.

The generations that came into adulthood in the sixties and seventies are still growing up. Ever since my generation entered the adult world, we have refused to get with the program. We reformed women's fashion—back then certain restaurants wouldn't let women wearing pants through the door. We challenged the conventional job categories for women—when the Help Wanted ads were separated by gender. We took charge of our economic lives—it's hard to believe that in those days a married woman had to get her husband's signature in order to take out a bank loan. We made ourselves heard in politics and business and the home. And we challenged ourselves to become the best we could be, despite a mountain of expert advice to conform and be grateful for whatever we got. Radical and conservative, daring and meek, we—and our younger contemporaries as well—have been imbued with confidence that "the program" can be changed. And with much turmoil and struggle, that is what we have been doing. So as we look ahead, every decade is as "new" as every decade has been so far for each of us.

Most of what we are doing, thinking, exploring is also new for the history of women's experience. We are the first generation to reach menopause with a life expectancy of another quarter of a century, with the know-how to be able to imagine making something of that time, with the support of the institutions and relationships we have built along the way. Our mothers and grandmothers understood the "change of life" as the time when their lives stopped changing. For many of them, those lives had pretty much been blocked out without their consultation; the primary variables for a woman were who would she marry, how would he treat her, how many children would she have, and how much or little hard luck would befall her. Not a very take-charge image. But the women's movement challenged that worldview in ways large and small. We learned from example and from experience that we had some control of our destiny and that, as has been said, we could become the men we wanted to marry.

Drew Gilpin Faust, who was fifty-nine when she became the first woman president of Harvard, is very accomplished, but also typical of her times. She grew up in rural Virginia in what she remembers as a "community of rigid racial segregation." Despite being "raised to be a rich man's wife," she rebelled against some (but, she adds, not all) of the demands of "a world where social arrangements were taken for granted and assumed to be time-less." Bryn Mawr, a women's college she attended in the sixties, gave muscle to her convictions. Her friend Mary Maples Dunn, who went on to become president of Smith, another of the great women's colleges, believes that all-female institutions "tended to give those young women a very good sense of themselves and encouraged them to develop their own ideas and to express themselves confidently" in a world where women were still "second-class citizens." Like most of us who have gained a degree of authority and self-confidence over the years, Faust's life didn't turn out the way it was supposed to. "One of the things that I think characterizes my generation—that characterizes me, anyway, and others of my generation—is that I've always been surprised by how my life turned out," she says now.

Every time we look up, there seems to be a new frontier ahead of us. We don't know where the next blow or blessing will come from; we don't know how we are going to deal with it, but increasingly we are gaining the confidence that we can cope with whatever comes. For me, to my amazement, a recent body blow was, of all things, the significance of a particular birthday.

Ever since Gloria Steinem's then-truly-shocking "This is what forty looks like!" I have totally endorsed her message: if each of us stops trying to hide our chronological years, we will liberate each benchmark for all of us. For years I talked the talk until I came upon a birthday that forced me to walk the walk.

For the occasion, my husband and a dear friend orchestrated the evening exactly as I wanted it—even though they would have preferred to do something a bit more elaborate. At my request, the ten guests brought a dish each had cooked, and we sat around our family dining room table toasting the chefs. I basked in the intimacy of the group: here were my two darling children, now old enough to offer in their tributes their own totally unexpected perspectives on my life. And my husband, with whom I have finally achieved a kind of wonderful equilibrium. (When I told someone that recently, he asked me how long it had taken. "About thirty-seven years," I replied.) There were three of my chosen friends, of twenty or more years. But also there was one new, or prospective, friend, someone I have a strong feeling is very special and hope to get to know better. A few others I wished could be there were away on adventures of their own—as it should be.

I felt pretty good about my life that night. And when I spent the rest of my birthday week with my then-ninety-year-old mother, I was reassured about how long it might go on like this. She doesn't look a day over seventy (the age at which she began studying for her Ph.D., which she completed in her early eighties, while holding a full-time job). She is "losing it" now but is still eager to go places and do things. In fact, the loss of short-term memory seems to make the world that much more full of surprises and wonder for her. Not a bad model for longevity.

So why is it that since that birthday, in circumstances where I happily volunteered my age in the past, I find myself obfuscating or downright lying?

I have spent several months trying to figure out what I am afraid of. Not death—at least not yet. Not looking older—I've gotten used to that. What I am afraid of is what I think my new age means to *others,* including other women who are experiencing their Second Adulthood but are a decade (or two) younger. I have been surprised and gratified by the way even women in their early forties have responded to my book *Inventing the Rest of Our Lives.* On several occasions a take-charge and worldly looking young woman has told me that she is buying two copies of the book, one for herself and one for her mother. For herself, she tells me, because although she is in the midst of making the necessary trade-offs in her stage of adulthood, she wants to glimpse ahead to where she may be able to retrieve some of the experiences she has to pass up now. For her mother, because her generation has forged a bond of truth telling with their mothers and they know their mothers need a little encouragement to get going on inventing the rest of their lives. I don't want to lose the camaraderie I feel with these forty-something women. I would hate to be dismissed as "the older generation" and shunted off their radar screens.

I'm thinking especially of the readers of *More* magazine, where I am a contributing editor. The magazine is for women over forty, which we all accept as a way of saying "older" but not "*old* old"—the age my mother is. But where is the crossover point? I am afraid that when the younger older women find out what birthday I have just celebrated, they will dismiss my ideas and my enthusiasm for this new stage of life as not relevant to theirs. And they will stop listening to me—or telling me how it is for them.

I don't want to be identified by my chronological age. Especially now, because I have so much to say about "aging." Before they jump to any conclusions, I want people to know something about my state of mind, to enter into conversation with me about experiences we share—"Yes, I know what she means" or "For me it is this way. . . ." I want to be seen for *who* I am, before anyone factors in what age I am.

Of course that is precisely why I *should* admit my age—to help demystify the arbitrary cutoff established by the Social Security Administration that I, too, used to see as separating one group from the rest of society. So here I go: I love where I am in my life—all sixty-five years of it so far!

There *are* some differences, though, between then, when at fifty I began experiencing wake-up calls to a new stage of life, and now, fifteen years into it. And if we could liberate our conversation from the numbers game, we could talk about those differences. The truth is: for me sixty isn't fifty. Not because of the milestones crossed but because of the territory that the woman who has lived those years has traversed during that time. What I can tell a fifty-year-old woman about my journey so far may be useful to her not when she hits sixty-five but when she hits a challenge that is similar to one I have met. While there are some constants—mainly physiological wear and tear—each woman's Second Adulthood trajectory is unique. Some of us go through menopause in our forties; others have children at the same age. Some of us find our work more satisfying with increased seniority and focus; others are looking to more personal aspects of their lives for renewal. Some are pulling out of long-standing relationships; others are getting in deeper. Some are feeling powerful waves of change; others hardly a ripple—yet. In the same way as no two women experience a given chronological age in the same way, any given woman is in flux as she moves along. Every day there are new affirmations of the insight *you are not who you were, only older.* Yes, you are older chronologically and physiologically, but you are younger in terms of time spent outgrowing who you were before you began figuring out some things.

If I am honest about the differences I am discovering as I move through my time, the truth of what I say will, I hope, enlarge the conversation we are having, not change the subject. So, a decade or so into my journey, if sixty is the new sixty, what is so new about it?

I'm beginning to see that many of the challenges I have been living with for a while have taken on a new light:

I'm beginning to see that the question, What am I going to do with the rest of my life? becomes less perplexing; it is actually answering itself.

I'm beginning to see that workplace issues recede as cosmic issues close in.

I'm beginning to see that my outlook is becoming a bit "darker," as one friend observed, but also less fearful.

I'm beginning to see that nothing is ever over—until it's all over.

I'm with poet and essayist Grace Paley, who "interviewed" herself for an essay she wrote entitled "Upstaging Time" when she was in her seventies. "Do you mind having to get older?" Interviewer asks. Paley doesn't answer directly, and instead goes on for pages enthusiastically answering related "questions" about her life, her friends, her work. Finally, she gives a straight (you would expect nothing less from Paley) answer: "By the way, my answer to your question is, I feel great. I like my life a lot. It is interesting every day. But it so happens I *do* mind."

What I am really describing as I wrestle with the differences and similarities between where I am and where other younger or older women are is the emergence of the notion of Horizontal Role Models, women who have been there, not chronologically but emotionally, psychologically, or experientially. A younger woman who had her children at an early age may have a lot to share about the empty nest; an older woman who is getting back into the job market may have important insights into the politics of the workplace. A cancer survivor of any age can help all of us focus on what is really important. And all of us can empathize with an attack of the what-am-I-doing blues.

The function of Horizontal Role Models in our lives is like that of a cluster of mothers who find themselves on adjoining benches at a playground: sharing tidbits of advice; commiserating about tiredness, body changes, the way the world sees them; fending off the suspicion each of them has that she is going crazy—and contributing to a rousing tide of knowing laughter. The chronological age of any one of them, or of the children they are tending, is irrelevant. Their bond is common experience. And the honesty with which they share it.

Our cadre of Horizontal Role Models is growing every minute. In the few years since we began the conversation about Second Adulthood, the first pioneers across that frontier have accumulated a track record of insights, resources, and anecdotes. Because of their spirit, they are role models for those who are following them. Because of the variability of each woman's adventure, they are ongoing role models and advisers for one another.

The one thing that can't be passed on is a one-size-fits-all pattern of challenges. As more women cut their own paths through the uncharted terrain of Second Adulthood, the terrain itself changes. The work/relationships/self juggling act never stops, but the weight and nature of the balls we are trying to keep in the air do change. Many of the issues that were paramount for women who turned fifty when I did—the trepidation about raising the subject of aging, the dearth of images we could relate to in advertising, the medical ignorance about our bodies—have modified and are somewhat different from the challenges confronting those crossing that threshold today. By the same token, the challenges and hot spots confronting the pioneers as they move further down the road are not what they were when they set out. Not only are you not aging the way you expected to (becoming an older version of who you were), but the evolutionary progress keeps on going, so that *you are not who you were* when you began this transition, either.

One of the ways some women measure their evolution is not by counting the years but by looking at where their mothers were at the same age. Marge Clauser, a poet and writer, writes poignantly about the legacy of limitations she has overcome:

> *My mother considered herself old when my father died in 1959.*
>
> *I came home from school one day and found her sitting at the kitchen table. She said, "I want to talk to you about getting married."*
>
> *My first thought was that she was talking about herself. However that didn't make sense. It only took a few seconds to realize that she viewed me as the prospective bride. I'd just turned 16, had never dated anyone seriously and I wanted to go to college. I voiced those facts.*
>
> *Her reply was, "Well, you need a man to take care of you because I'm not going to be around to do it in the future."*
>
> *My father had been ill for years before his death, so I immediately asked "Are you sick?"*
>
> *She said, "No. I'm old." She was only 52.*
>
> *Mom then said she wanted to make sure I knew where she kept some important items. She showed me where she*

*kept an insurance policy and other papers. Then she showed
me her burial dress. It was pink and gray lace over a taffeta
slip—so unlike anything I'd ever seen her wear that I was
speechless.*

*She zipped the dress back into its plastic garment bag.
There it stayed, moving with her to five different states over
the next 26 years, until she died at age 78. Getting ready for
her funeral, I took the dress out of the back of her closet and
unzipped the garment bag. The dress immediately began
to disintegrate. It ended up as a pile of pink and gray dust,
resembling ashes.*

Marge had initially followed her mother's advice and married
very young, but when she became a widow at twenty-nine with
"two small children and no education," she made a major choice:
"not to follow Mom's example any longer." She didn't want to
invest the rest of her life in a disintegrating lace dress. Instead
she got her high school and college degrees, married—this time
to the "love of my life" who had three children of his own. She
now has fifteen grandchildren. Over the years she worked as a
health-care administrator, an innkeeper, a city commissioner,
and a board member before becoming a writer. Now, at the age
her mother was when she gave up, Marge can say, "This is *my*
prime time!"

"My mother literally spent over twenty-five years waiting to
die," Marge says sadly. "Her life could have and should have been
so different." And then she pays tribute to the Horizontal Role
Models in her life who are helping confirm her more positive
outlook. "I meet women my age and older living vital, interesting
lives, in spite of health and financial concerns. The difference

between our Second Adulthood and my mother's is we stay as active as possible, especially mentally. Never stop learning new things, listening to new ideas, meeting new people."

As each of us moves into this new stage of life, there are literally more of us sharing the experience. More of us comfortable enough with what is happening to reassure one another that "you are not alone" and you are definitely not "crazy" for embracing change. More of us to define the "new" fifty and sixty and seventy. More of us to change by example and by activism the image of women like us in our society. Polls suggest that we are feeling pretty good about how it is going. One study found that 46 percent of women in their fifties say they are "extremely" or "very satisfied" with their overall wellness; the percentage increased to 50 percent among those in their sixties and to 66 percent of those in their seventies.

The obsession in the media, the pharmaceutical industry, the medical establishment, and the youth business with the menace of menopause often drowns out the positive message from other women who are living the changes. People around her—family, doctors, employers—and a woman herself can all too easily dismiss her unsettled state as the onset of hormonal hysteria. Make no mistake about it, this is the onset of something much more meaningful.

The hallmark of the beginning of Second Adulthood is a necessary but disturbing descent into what I call the Fertile Void. Like the onset of menopause, this profound upheaval has nothing to do with chronological age. It may coincide with the loss of biological fertility and it may take as long or longer than a pregnancy, but the similarities end there. The Fertile Void is a place of confusion in which a midlife woman wanders without a map until she finds her new self. During her sojourn there, she will lose her way more than once and she will encounter the modern-day—and female—versions of the medieval dragons that tested the knights of yore.

Of all the experiences I have compared with women who are growing up alongside me, the Fertile Void is the most universal. Every woman describes it in similar terms: "I don't know what's happening." "I can't get my act together." "I can't see my way out of this." And "What is taking so long?" They are desperately trying to find the way out of a disconcerting state of not-knowing and imagine that the key lies in the answer to The Question (What am I going to do with the rest of my life?). The problem is that before any woman can get to the rest of it, she has to figure out what she means by "my life."

No wonder the typical sojourn in the Fertile Void takes so long and feels so maddeningly unpredictable. Like the proverbial river, you can't push the Fertile Void; it is an organic process that defies the tools that have served us so well at other points in our lives. At first, we assume we will be able to multitask our way through it: make a list, consult experts, fit it into the schedule. Not so. For one thing, multitasking is one of the skills that dull with age. But more important, the months-long stretch of doubt, confusion, and experimentation defies efficiency and goal setting. Women in the midst of it share stories of free fall and seemingly random events—and serendipitous sparks: the impulsive decision to try eating alone at a restaurant that leads to a new and guiding friendship; the night school course that kindles a new interest; the exercise regimen that builds new goals as well as new muscles; the overheard conversation that switches on a lightbulb. In the process of moving among such fragments of experience, we lose control of our lives—if we ever really had it. We feel clumsy, and we mess up. It is important to cut ourselves a little slack—not easy for women who have practically invented the unforgiving to-do list and all-encompassing standards-and-practices agenda; it will all go better if we are less impatient and demanding of our own performance.

Nearly everyone eventually gets through the Fertile Void and lands on her feet. That is the first piece of wisdom confirmed by our Horizontal Role Models. But you won't end up where you thought you would. That is the second. The promise of moving ahead is not a crisp new game plan for the rest of your life. It is a more dynamic and incomplete *travel* plan: the profound sense that you are on the road to understanding what matters—to you.

Here is Lynda's account of her time in the limbo of the Fertile Void:

> *At my fiftieth birthday three years ago I knew things were beginning to stir for me, but it was all too vague at the time. I went on a yoga retreat with my oldest and best friend and we celebrated our milestone birthdays together, but it didn't come together for me until much later.*
>
> *Nine months ago I decided to leave my high-power executive role. People thought I was crazy, but I knew I needed to get back in touch with what I really wanted to do, but was not sure exactly what that was. All I knew for sure was that I no longer wanted to continue with the role I was in. I wanted my personal freedom, and time, just the pure pleasure of time.*

After nine months of not doing anything career-oriented, focusing on fixing up my house, doing little decorating projects I'd put off for years, cleaning out closets, taking some short trips abroad, having lunch with my girlfriends for the first time in many years, doing some cooking, enjoying my kids, I suddenly understood what I wanted to do. I gave birth to myself—again. I realize that what I want to do next, and actually shocked myself and the people around me, I want to combine everything I've loved about my two prior careers and bring together those aspects that I want to continue doing and drop those aspects I don't enjoy and bring it all together for my culminating Act Three.

Other milestones almost as common as the Fertile Void are beginning to emerge as some of us report back from the road ahead. If the Horizontal Role Models were to put captions to snapshots of their journey so far, they would be these:

RECALIBRATING OUR PLACE IN THE WORLD: As the passions that will drive the choices ahead emerge, our priorities change. A reconsideration of What Matters going forward shuffles the deck. With increasing clarity about what we need to do for ourselves, we find that our relationships with others need some adjustments. In terms of work ambition, productivity, professional commitment, the future looks different on the other side of the Fertile Void.

A LONGING TO LET GO AND MAKE PEACE: As the pieces of self-knowledge and self-determination begin to fall into place, we are inspired to get rid of old baggage, including resentments, disappointments, extravagant expectations, and move on with what we've found worth holding on to.

A SENSE OF MASTERY: Working from our strengths makes it possible to see the way toward making changes and taking risks. With each risk taken, our self-confidence builds until we realize that we have established a track record: we can handle what life throws us—good and bad. The message is "I am in charge of me."

AN AWAKENING OF AUTHENTICITY: Throughout our lives, we have taken on so many roles. So many imposed expectations. So many responsibilities we weren't sure we could—or wanted to—handle. So many doubts about performance. Now the scripted lines are giving way to the sound of each woman's own voice, with the words to tell the truth as she sees it. The defiance and daring that are precipitating so much change bring us closer to who we want to be.

That defiance and daring are the source of everyone's personal favorite: **BEHAVING BADLY.** The repertoire of outspoken, outrageous, and downright mischievous behavior that each of us has been building since the first winds of change hit is so liberating that I have named the mind-set behind it the Fuck-You Fifties.

As Horizontal Role Models, we are all—adult women of any age—empowering one another. Along the way we are accumulating Life Lessons for Growing Up, sharing them and celebrating where they are taking us. You will hear from many of them in this book.

Deb, for one. Unlike Marge, whose mother was an anti–role model, Deb came to value her mother's advice when she got to a point where she could make it happen for herself. An essay she wrote about turning fifty reflects the humor, daring, and honesty that characterize the discovery process we are going through.

I remember my mom saying to me on her forty-fifth birthday, "It gets better as you get older." Yeah, right! I thought she was nuts. I was a smug 23 year old. She was just beginning her dance with middle age and she was famous for her mood swings. She used to chase the kids around the house with a fly swatter. I remember feeling sorry for her and thinking she had to say things like that, to make herself feel better, an affirmation of sorts. She certainly could not believe it! She had a fridge magnet that said "over 40 and feeling foxy." It made me just cringe. C'mon this was my MOM! Well, guess what? My mom's gone but her magnet has the place of honor on my fridge. And guess what else? I'm over 50 and feeling foxy.

I don't want to look, feel or be 20, 30, or even 40 ever again! A hard body and fresh face is not worth the struggles those years bring; the self-doubt, the constant comparisons, the need to fit in, to measure up, be as good as. I'll take this age any day! I've found that what I lose on the outside I gain on the inside.

Sure my hormones are raging, but instead of seeing this as a negative experience, I look at it as an opportunity to hear what my body is saying and fix what needs to be fixed. I've cleaned up my act. I quit drinking and began paying attention to what I put into my body. In fact, I begin to respect my body.

I've made some significant changes in my life. I stopped putting all my eggs in everyone else's baskets and began to fill my own. I discovered I have a creative spirit and initiated many projects that have filled my life with joy and prosperity.

Despite all the craziness I feel good. Happy. Sure of myself. Completely the opposite of the scared 13 year old I was when I first began to fill up with hormones. Now, on the other side of the river I am self-possessed. I have a strong sense of faith, of who I am. I accept myself, all of it, good and bad. It's a nice place to be.

Deb's description of her new-found "faith," resonates for me; it helps explain why in the midst of so much questioning and seeming chaos, I find a sense of peace—a stasis within motion. And why it is that I feel so strongly that no matter how many years I accumulate, I am not moving away from the experience of Second Adulthood that I share with other women at different chronological points in their lives. We have so much in common. For one thing, we are learning to thrive on paradox. Even though we keep re-creating familiar patterns (despite our efforts to change some of them), we also feel we are breaking out of old constraints. As much as we long to set goals, we feel more alive when we are reconsidering them. The more we are in flux, the more grounded we feel. The further we get from who we were, the closer we feel we are getting to who we are.

The sense of going around in circles is a frustrating symptom of the Fertile Void, but those circles look very different in later stages. They become a spiral—a circle plus change. The specifics are different for each of us at each moment along the way, but the momentum and the constellations of shared experience create a magnetic field in which we can exchange understanding and encouragement. As I look down from my ride, I see the reassuring constants gathered over my sixty-five years as well as the maturing trajectory of my new self. My view is illuminated by the electrons of energy from the lives and experiences of the women who are out here in this new galaxy with me.

THE LESSON: No matter how many messages we get urging us to act our age, what we need to do is act our *stage:* to follow the promptings of that restless, curious, daring, and doubtful voice that begins to speak up as we move out of our first adulthood. Annual birthdays—particularly the milestones that society measures us by—are for gifts, but are meaningless for situating yourself in your life. Wherever you may be now, you won't be there long and you won't be that same "you" for very long either. "Older" doesn't explain the unique ferment of the Fertile Void, where, no matter what birthday you are marking, your journey begins. While it is your own remarkable journey, you can count on other women to keep you company along the way.

Lesson Two

Nothing Changes
if Nothing Changes

The only thing that makes life possible is permanent, intolerable uncertainty—not knowing what comes next.

—Ursula K. Le Guin

S econd Adulthood is all about change—the changes that befall us and those we generate. The first without the second creates a miasma of disappointment. The second, if it doesn't incorporate the first, is frustrating and discouraging.

A restlessness that creates a nonspecific itch to make changes is behind much of our seemingly random and unpredictable behavior. That urge to bring new elements into the mix of our lives, combined with a simultaneous desire to revise our established lifestyle, throws us off balance a lot of the time. Sometimes it is like falling down Alice's rabbit hole: you don't know which end is up. The free fall into the Fertile Void is alternately exhilarating and terrifying; any guideposts to help set your course when you emerge are few and far between, and there are no timetables for any changes that you make from there on. The only imperative of the transition from the society-defined stages for women into the unprecedented and unexplored next stage is that each of us can—nay, *must*—begin to write her own script. Each player is unique. There are no roles. (There are no white knights either.) Some people catch fire with passion for a new life and others putt-putt along making small but very meaningful course adjustments. The changes need not be as dramatic as parachuting out of a plane or as operatic as running off with the cable guy, but they will probably feel as momentous.

Not long ago I joined twenty midlife women who had gotten together to ponder the question: What will I do with the rest of my life? Someone asked for a show of hands from those who had a dream or a passion they couldn't wait to get to. Only two hands went up, and the rest of us looked on enviously. How, we worried, could we move forward if we couldn't identify a driving force: like the desire to write a novel or start a business or to sail around the world by balloon? As we commiserated, those of us with no grand passion heard ourselves admit to inner voices that whisper, "Do this" and simmering interests that are heating up now that we are letting ourselves reconsider What Matters in our lives; we just didn't consider them big enough ideas. Those less torrid impulses are simply a different source of guidance: a pilot light. A flame that doesn't consume but doesn't burn out either, it literally pilots us through the shoals and currents of our new stage of life.

A pilot light of any intensity is ignited by discarding shoulda-woulda-coulda thinking. That includes accumulated baggage, especially expectations—about yourself, about others, about how your life is "supposed" to be. So what if you have never been an outdoor person? So what if you have always been counted on to take the minutes at a meeting? So what if you have always been so dignified? So what if you have gone to work in an office every day of your life? That was then. Now is now. Once the unnecessary carry-on is set down, it is much easier to take off into the wild blue yonder.

Which is not necessarily a literal recommendation. While some women can redesign their lives from top to bottom—and keep on doing it—most of us can only manage small changes at first. Going back to school can be too big an undertaking right now; try exchanging a regular TV show for the crossword puzzle every night. Opening a craft store would be fun, but maybe all you can handle for the moment is a pair of knitting needles and an evening at the local yarn shop with others in the same boat. Quitting an oppressive job may be a necessary objective, but getting a wardrobe together for the job search may revise your self-image, which can make taking a life-changing risk imaginable. Moreover, changing the metabolism of your days is not only about adding on experiences; it may be just as much of a healthy shake-up to pull back from a time commitment, an emotional involvement, or a long-standing responsibility. The change can even be a one-time thing. I know a woman who dared herself to sign up for a Harley motorcycle course for women over forty. She did, and she loved it. But, she says, she'd never do it again. "Just driving a motorcycle that one time set me free!" Big or small, moving forward or retreating, a change of any kind gets the currents moving.

For many women I meet it comes as a great relief to be reassured that even if "they" are all doing "it" one way, and even if the magazine articles are all extolling those examples, if it doesn't feel right to you, *you don't have to do it.* Many of the most frequently offered suggestions for getting on with your life call for what could, for you, mean throwing the baby out with the bathwater; others are just too big, too costly, or in some way undoable. So for those of us with more modest daring, here are some of the **Things You Don't Have to Do** (though it may turn out that you want to, after all) in order to find your pilot light:

- **Leave Your Job:** Many women sense a loss of professional drive as they move toward their fifties and worry that there is something wrong with them. But it may just be that you have reached a job that suits you or that you are ready to shift gears from climbing the ladder to settling on a plateau of accomplishment. (A recent survey found that among workers older than fifty-five, 59 percent say they are "satisfied" or "extremely satisfied" with their jobs, nearly a third more than any of the younger groups.)

- **Leave Your Partner:** In fact, changes are taking place in both partners that may make couples more compatible now than they have ever been. For one thing, among heterosexual couples our hormonal balances are shifting toward each other—testosterone, in particular. For another, age brings a certain mellowness to both men and women. But best of all, many men and women find themselves experiencing a renewed curiosity about themselves and, in the course of reviewing the choices they have made, experiencing renewed curiosity in the partner they thought they knew so well.

- **Leave the Country:** The most commonly voiced all-purpose passion is travel. But many women don't really want to leave their (newly empty) nests; instead they want to feather them with cozy experiences and new-found intimacy. Others may want to make more internal, spiritual journeys. And still others may find that their communities hold unexplored wonders and possibilities, say, running for office.

- **Leave Your Senses:** Learning to scuba dive, taking up Chinese, or moving into a yurt may sound like just the high-intensity transformation you need, but you may also find that taking tango lessons, putting together a family tree, or planning a cousins' reunion becomes the first step toward the rest of your life.

- **Leave Your Body:** Sure, it would be great to lose those twenty pounds, and it might feel very daring to let the gray grow in or get plastic surgery. On the other hand, that might make you feel less like your true self than you do now. Only you can tell which it is. Maybe a regular pedicure or a new hair style will be all the transformation you need. Our bodies are the front line in the confrontation with aging, but when the showdown is getting nasty, just imagine how many good laughs we would miss if our bodies weren't giving us so much hilarious material.

A common problem is that we defeat ourselves before we start by replacing old unrealistic expectations with new ones. Even though there is no program for making change, we keep trying to pin down the moment when change is happening, or set a specific goal for when it should happen. We simply push too hard, wasting energy in an effort to impose certainty on discovery. And we want it all right away. It is almost impossible to accept the notion that drift may be the only way into the magnetic field where the pieces of this confusing transition come together.

"Only bad things happen quickly . . . phone calls in the night, accidents, conversations with doctors bearing awful news," writes psychiatrist Dr. Gordon Livingston in *Too Soon Old, Too Late Smart*. "In fact," he points out, "apart from a last-second touchdown, unexpected inheritance, winning the lottery, or a visitation from God, it is hard to imagine sudden good news. Virtually all the happiness-producing processes in our lives take time, usually a long time: Learning new things, changing old behaviors, building satisfying relationships, raising children. This is why patience and determination are among life's primary virtues."

Many women report that it took a year or more drifting around in the Fertile Void before they began to feel a sense of purpose. By then, though, they had found out something they hadn't expected: that making the journey is where the real action is.

Here is one of countless accounts I've heard of how it feels to find your whole life in motion and how little use the best-laid plans often are. "Several months ago, I made the decision to quit my full-time job that I've held for twenty-two years and work fewer hours," Barb told me with a mixture of pride and trepidation. Her response to that impulsive—and liberating—act was, typically, mixed. "As soon as the decision was made I second-guessed myself, wondering, 'What in the world made me decide to do that?'" Then the ground shifted under her feet. "My employer decided that I wouldn't be as much of an asset part-time as I am now." Instead of half a job, she had no job. By the time her game plan dematerialized, she had pulled up anchor on her life and despite the cold waters, she was not as pan-icky as she would have predicted she would be; instead Barb felt strangely exhilarated. "I don't know what I will do—I do need some sort of part-time work financially as well as just to stay active in society, but I am looking forward to the restruc-turing and new adventures it will lead to."

"Is there anything as horrible as starting on a trip?" writes Anne Morrow Lindbergh in *Gift from the Sea,* with a down-to-earth understanding of how hard it is to plunge into the unknown. "Once you're off that's all right, but the last moments are earthquake and convulsion and the feeling that you are a snail being pulled off your rock." We have all felt like that snail at some point in our current travels. But the bottom line is, action trumps brooding: you've simply got to *do* something! It doesn't matter what step you take or what direction you start out in; once you do it, you are on the road—to wherever.

What *does* matter—very much—is the deceptively simple insight that nothing changes, if nothing changes. This phrase changed the life of a woman gambling addict who was about as lost as anyone I know of. "Absolutely nothing could keep me away from 'the fix,'" Mary wrote in Marlo Thomas's second collection of life-changing moments, *The Right Words at the Right Time.* "When the compulsion hit, it took me over com-pletely. I'd be vacuuming the floor one minute, and then the next, the urge would be so strong I'd leave the vacuum cleaner right where it was, still plugged in, jump in the car, and go. My two sons, nine and fifteen, would cry and beg me to stay home, but I couldn't." She attended Gamblers Anonymous meetings, but she couldn't kick the habit. Then at one meeting, she writes, someone looked her in the eye and said, "Nothing changes, if nothing changes." The moment I read that phrase I felt I had found the words to convey the important message women like me needed to hear. And when Mary went on to admit that it took another year before she could act on that message, I was sure it would speak to anyone feeling lost in the Fertile Void.

Another way of looking at the power of the smallest change is to compare our efforts to move our snail self off the rock to what scientists call the "butterfly effect," the theory that the flutter of a butterfly wing somewhere in the world can, as a Wikipedia contributor put it, "create tiny changes in the atmosphere that ultimately cause a tornado to appear (or, for that matter, prevent a tornado from appearing)."

Every woman I talked to has found herself in Lindbergh's snail mode at some point; the extremely diverse encounters with common sticking points lend themselves to a kind of Horizontal Role Models' catalog of ways to look at whatever version of stuck you are experiencing. I've paired each piece of advice with its opposite to underscore the point that there is no right way to get moving, and that there can never be a one-size-fits-any-two-women, let alone an all-women Guide to Change.

Fear

We each have our personal demons that show up in the middle of the night shrieking a litany of worst-case scenarios: What if I don't have enough money to support myself? What if that nagging ache is something really serious? What if I can't figure out what to do next? What's *wrong* with meeeeeee?! They can drain our waking resolve.

- **Tell your Demons to Shut up.** I had a friend who literally did that—out loud!—whenever she awoke full of doubts and self-pity. Another woman dismisses those panicky voices with a sarcastic "Thanks for sharing." A stern "mommy voice" may come in handy here.
- **Engage Just One Demon.** The conversations that take place in the dark night of the soul can be transformative. Single out just one of the fears that bring on a cold sweat. And stare it down. Finding a new financial adviser to review your "dire" situation, switching medications for a chronic medical condition, or instituting a weekly let-it-all-hang-out lunch with two or three open, lively women should silence at least one of the voices of doom. At least temporarily.

Risks

Risk taking is one of the bywords of this stage, but like everything else risk means different things to different women. Think of the impulse to dare as a yearning to explore the road not taken.

- **Go for it!** Sign up for that trek into a rain forest. Propose yourself for a promotion. Try out for a play. Start your own business. Run for office. Or simply move the furniture around or repaint the dingy green walls that have been depressing you for years.
- **Conserve Your Resources.** For you, the road not taken— the one that is overgrown with menacing vines—may in fact be the graded and paved one. The road forward

may, in fact, be heading in the opposite direction from where you have been heading. Dare to be conservative. Shift your finances, for example, from playing the market to long-term planning; or give your knees a rest from marathon running and take up tai chi; or cut back from a seventy-hour work week and see what serendipity seeps into that vacuum.

Work

One of the things *you don't have to do* is quit your job, but you may want to. How do you know?

- **Picture a New Job.** Career consultant Carole Hyatt, who is very good at helping people get unstuck professionally, has devised an exercise that I find especially liberating. She asks clients to list all the skills they have, as they have done a thousand times before. Then she shakes it all up by telling each client to cross off the skills she hates. What? You mean I don't have to keep doing something just because I am good at it? I can look for a job that just uses the skills I love? That is really mind-blowing.

- **Make Your Work Your Safe Haven.** There was a time when I was dragging myself to work, because everything at home was in disarray. Several of my coworkers were in the same boat. We decided to form a Thank God It's Monday club to affirm the fact that at least in the office we could find recognition for a job well done. It's often easier to contemplate changing your job than changing your marriage or your life style or yourself. But maybe your job is what's working for you, so leave it be—for now.

Plans

Our first recourse when confronted with a challenge is to reach for a pencil and paper. We secretly believe that a to-do list will fend off the evil eye. But the lists themselves can be a source of discouragement and stuckness: "If nothing on the list of Things I Always Wanted to Do appeals to me, I must be a lazy slug who belongs on a rock." Wrong. You just aren't the person who wrote that list anymore. In fact, the list-making mode itself can hold you back. Unless you reinvent it.

- **A Master Plan.** Focus on one project, one that really gets your juices going—an exotic vacation, for example, or a new garden—and build a countdown into your appointment book for the next twelve months: send for catalogs on the third Wednesday in January, block out an itinerary/flower layout on the same day in February, check airfares/order seeds in March, and so on. Check off the items to keep the momentum going.

- **Unplan.** For those of us who try to control events by planning for them, the breakthrough is to let the chips fall where they may. Among those chips, an event that might have "ruined" a carefully laid plan can be a delicious surprise. When methodical thinking is submerged, creative thinking rises to the surface. To lay the groundwork for this laid-back approach, practice canceling at least one appointment a week, watch random TV (I'm told the cooking channel is the next best thing to LSD in terms of freeing up the imagination), work out without music, don't check your e-mail until an hour later than usual.

Speaking Up

One of life's delightful and empowering discoveries these days is the sound of a new voice: your own. We are just beginning to listen to ourselves ("I don't care what people think" is often followed by the clarification "I care more and more what *I* think"). It takes a little practice to recognize the timbre of that voice and the narrative that is taking shape.

- **Talk to Yourself.** Even if you never kept a diary as a teenager, you may get hooked on venting the paranoid insights and petty gripes you are ashamed to admit to anyone else, the smoldering resentments, lingering disappointments, and unspeakable fears that are bubbling up in response to the big question, What am I going to do with the rest of my life? A journal is the place to tell the naked truth—to yourself. Getting it on the page, as Julia Cameron points out in *The Artist's Way,* also gets rid of the stuff that "muddies our days."

- **Listen to the World Around You.** Sometimes an audit of your life balance sheet results in an unexpected return. Keeping a "gratitude journal" is a sort of glass-half-full accounting. Each day you write down the heart-warming things that happened to you. Recently I was given one with the promise it would help me stop and take notice of "the small and big moments along your life path that give you joy." The inviting little spiral-bound book offered sample entries for the beginner: "I returned it—and with no questions got my money back." "I heard that song and for the first time, it didn't make me sad." And "she actually said, 'Thanks Mom.'"

Remodeling

Habits. Why does the word always pair up with *bad*? After all, habits get us through the day, but they can hold us back too. As a yoga teacher once told me about a certain posture that never felt right, "Bad habits make you rigid. And then when life throws you a curve, you can't handle it so well." Being flexible applies to how we evaluate the habits that R Us.

- **That's Just Who I Am.** Find a flaw you always meant to fix—like laughing very loud or waving your hands when you speak or a chronically unmade bed—and reconsider it. Maybe it works for today's you. Or not wasting the time and energy trying to change it is what works for you. So stop apologizing and incorporate that idiosyncrasy into your table of contents, and move on to finding and exercising something you like about yourself.

- **That's Not Who I Want to Be Anymore.** Perhaps you are ready to become tidy, to learn how to "modulate," lighten up or get more serious. Even lose five pounds. It might be fun to become a master of the wok after a lifetime of being an aficionado of Chinese takeout.

Other People

One of the big changes that come with age is the reduced priority we give to playing well with others. Psychologists find that in general we become less dependent on the reassurance of being part of a group: a social circle, a professional organization, even a family. On the other hand, there are activities that we once took pride in going solo—travel comes to mind—that have become more fun now, or more convenient, when others are along for the ride. It may well be that you have become more sociable in some ways and more reclusive in others.

- **Join a Group.** Maybe you have more time on your hands—now that the kids are in school full time, now that you are divorced, now that you've stopped coloring your hair. Even if you were never a joiner, see how it feels. Sign up for a night school course. Volunteer for a political campaign. Join a sketch class.
- **Quit a Group.** Perhaps you agreed to be secretary of the library association or signed up for the course in Spanish because you felt you "ought to." Now you realize your time is too precious and you would rather—can you believe it?—be alone. The poet Marianne Moore wrote: "The best cure for loneliness is solitude." Try it.

Me, Me, Me

All this self-discovery takes more time and attention than we are used to devoting to ourselves. That will have to change. The restless curiosity that is so unsettling is part of a growing imperative to sort out who you are becoming from who you have been. It is a drive for authenticity. The destination, as Judy Garland is reported to have said, is to "always be a first-rate version of yourself, rather than a second-rate version of somebody else."

- **Get "Selfish."** Putting yourself first simply means putting yourself up there alongside everyone else. One woman calls it "getting out of the emotional management business." Scale back the intensity of your sensitivity to every nuance of mood, your anticipation of every need, and your desire to solve every problem for those you love and spend some quality time with your own moods, needs, and problems.

- **Get Generous.** If you have been a hard-driving work/family juggler, you may have lost touch with your larger generosity. You may be poised to find joy in fostering in others what you are beginning to achieve in your own life: freedom, self-discovery, sharing. Mentoring on a formal or volunteer basis, or simply paying closer attention to the young people in your life, is a way of discovering—by putting yourself in a position to pass it on—what you know about the world.

All these tricks of the trade for making change can do is pry your inner snail off the rock. The rest—"not knowing what comes next," as Le Guin says—is "what makes life possible." You cannot assume anything about yourself, now or in the future, based on what has gone before. What mattered then may not matter at all now. What was feasible then may not be feasible now. At any point, life may intervene and change everything. But you will be able to take from all those revisions and reversals what you need to go forward.

Maryl could never have imagined that an unwanted birthday present would ultimately ignite her pilot light, the flickering and subdued but steady beacon that would guide her from "there" to "here." She was a management consultant, and her husband, Bill, a Peace Corps executive. There were times when they lived halfway around the world from each other, especially when their son, who was chronically ill, was young, with Maryl remaining in the States while Bill took extended research trips overseas. They now live together in one of the republics of the former Soviet Union.

I have loved art since I was very young. I've always gone to art museums, art exhibits—I was passionate about Picasso—art wasn't anything that I did myself, but it was something that I absolutely loved. Photography, on the other hand, was of no interest to me. Bill would always take pictures when we traveled and he always took pictures of the family, and that was his thing and it was fine.

Then for one birthday—it must have been around my fiftieth—he gave me this present, which I opened and to my astonishment it was a camera. I couldn't believe it, because it was like the last thing on earth that I would ever want. I thanked him; I took a roll of film, and I put the camera away. The next year for my birthday, he gave me a bigger and better camera, and I was like shocked! I thanked him, and I took a roll of film, looked at the pictures, and never touched the camera again. And the third year he gave me this huge—I mean I thought it was huge then—really terrific Nikon camera, and I thanked him, but I didn't know what to make of it. I now had three cameras in my closet, never intending to touch any of them.

Okay, now I have to fast forward several years to when

we moved from one house to another. Bill had been going to Africa a lot for his work, and he would come home with these fantastic African sculptures, but because of the way our house was at the time, we'd put them away up in the attic. When we moved to this new house we could actually display the African sculptures, and when we displayed them I realized that I couldn't remember where any of them were from. So I said to Bill, "You know, for my winter project I think what I'd like to do is take pictures of these and put the names of where they're from and something about these sculptures, what do you think?" And he said, "Great idea."

So I got out this Nikon camera, set it up in this empty room in the new house and went to photograph the first African sculpture. I held up the camera to take a picture of the sculpture, and I knew from what I could see in the viewfinder that I would not like this picture. So I went downstairs and I said to Bill, you know I really think I should have a macro lens for this camera. He was out the door, and within an hour he was back with this macro lens that I absolutely loved, and I spent the whole winter photographing those African sculptures. I did not love photographing, but I loved something about this, it's sort of like if I love talking to you it doesn't mean I love the telephone or want to be a telephone operator—right?

At the end of that winter I noticed in the Washington Post *that there was a note about a Day Lily Day at the American Horticultural Society garden, and I thought, my god if I can see all these details in these African sculptures with this macro lens, I bet if I used it for flowers it would be fantastic. I've always loved flowers, so that was a pretty natural thing for me. I called the AHS and asked them if they would mind if I came and photographed the day lilies on Day Lily Day—I had never even been to this place—and the woman said to me, "Not only would we be glad for you to, but we'd be interested in your photographs." I had now taken all of thirty-six pictures of these African sculptures, and this woman is saying she'd be interested in my photos. Well, Day Lily Day comes and I go out to this garden, and there are these huge number of varieties of day lilies, more than I'd ever seen, I mean I'd seen these yellow and orange ones along the road, but they had tons—so many varieties. So I took all of these very careful pictures of their day lilies.*

Later, I called this woman; she said, "Oh, I remember you; we're too busy now, call me in a month." I called her in a month, she said, "I'll call you," and then I just forgot about it because that's like what we all say when we don't want to be bothered. Lo and behold in November she called me back and she said, "We'd like to see your pictures of the day lilies."

I take my slide projector out there, and when I arrive and she said, "There's a big meeting going on; nobody can be here to look at the pictures except me, do you mind if we do this in the kitchen?" I had to swallow my pride, and we went in the kitchen. I flicked on the first slide, and then I flicked on the second slide, and she said, "Wait a minute." She left and came back with the director and several of the staff, and they spent the next two hours looking at the pictures, and then said they wanted to publish them in their magazine, they wanted to sell them in their shop,

and da-da-da-da-da-da, and that was the beginning of my
photography.

Maryl went on to have several shows of her work and to move
into new technology and new subject matter. "When we moved
to Egypt, I decided to explore what I could do with a computer.
The result was that I was able to create unique images, unlike
any that had been taken in Egypt because I could create layers,
like the layers of civilization and the layers of culture and reli-
gion that exist there. That was a major breakthrough for me."

There was also an emotional vein to this story. At first the
photography was therapy of a sort, a pilot light in the darkness
of her grief. Ultimately it became a skill and, yes, a passion.
"I did the photographs of the African sculptures one winter
shortly after our son died," remembers Maryl heavily. "I could
do that solitary project in our home, totally alone, which was
what I needed. My pursuing photography by taking macro
photographs of flowers was also a very special way for me to
be engaged with something new, but solitary, which is what I
was continually seeking. I was acutely aware of the fact that the
beauty of my photographs was in stark contrast to the black hole
that I was experiencing daily."

Every change is a risk. But the alternative to this kind of risk
is not safety, but lost opportunity. The challenge from a condition of uncertitude and tentativeness is to let go of the game-
plan mentality we know so well and simply meander across the
new terrain one unsure step at a time.

THE LESSON: While we know that we want to get on
with finding out what we will do with the rest of our lives, we

are afraid to take those first steps into the unknown and risk destabilizing our status quo. Nothing short of a shake-up will relieve the frustration and confusion. The good news is that any action—large or small, proactive or reactive, affirming or denying—will make *something* happen. Scale up. Scale down. Acquire. Discard. Give. Take. Whatever act seems most doable is the one to start with. You can always change your mind. You probably will. But by the time you do, you will have begun to build momentum. It doesn't matter what we change first or even whether that change will make any difference in the long run. Anything that gets you moving will help get you where you need to be.

No Is Not a Four-Letter Word

When I stand up for myself and my beliefs, they call me a bitch.
When I stand up for those I love, they call me a bitch.
When I speak my mind, think my own thoughts or do things
    my own way, they call me a bitch.
Being a bitch means I won't compromise what's in my heart.
It means I live my life MY way.
It means I won't allow anyone to step on me.
When I refuse to tolerate injustice and speak against it, I am
    defined as a bitch.
. . . I am outspoken, opinionated and determined.
. . . And if that makes me a bitch, so be it. I embrace the title
    and am proud to bear it.

—"Bitchology," circulated on the Internet

To adapt the immortal words of Kermit the Frog, it's not easy being a bitch. Standing up to power, which is what saying no is, is an act of supreme courage for most women. Many of us grew up afraid of the word, both as a statement *by* us and as a reply *to* us. Nice girls were supposed to say yes—except to sex, of course. People who say yes are liked; I wanted to be liked. By the same token, I deduced that a no from someone meant they *didn't* like me—not just my request or my opinion, but my whole self.

Given such high stakes, it is no wonder that talking back was not an insignificant act. (I don't think men will ever understand this about us.) An ill-advised rebellion could be costly. Stepping out of line might result in emotional wipeout or humiliation; physical retaliation was another possibility that could be immediate and even life-threatening. The economic consequences for a woman who had no source of income—other than the man she answered to—were an ever-present threat. Even today statistics show that fear of getting a no keeps women from asking for raises as often as men do, and as a result, reinforces historic salary discrepancies.

It is a truism that you won't get what you want if you don't ask for it, but we are learning that saying please is not the only way to get it. Many women are stunned to discover that a common reply to a no is a bewildered, "I never knew you felt that way about it."

For Madeline* the catalyst was not her own no but her husband's to her decision to go to graduate school:

> *My husband informed me that he wasn't going to support my efforts, meaning that he wasn't going to co-sign for my loan, or support my efforts in any way.*

---

*Denotes a pseudonym throughout.

I kind of "fell back" and thought Okay, so it's just not my time. I'll wait until the boys are finished with college; then I'll go.

Then it happened. The "fuck you fifties" kicked in, even though I was 48. I told my husband I didn't need him to support or co-sign; I'd do it on my own. THIS IS NOT THE WAY I HAVE OPERATED FOR THE PAST 25 YEARS. I was a stay-at-home mom and hubby did the finances. I had always been fine with this, but not any more.

I made out the applications and thought "I do not know how I am going to do this time-wise if I work and money-wise if I don't. Hubby thinks it's not the right time, so we'll probably fight constantly."

I got in the graduate program. I got offered a research position that paid for tuition. I got financing. My husband all of a sudden changed his mind when he saw I wasn't going to change mine. Again I have never ever done anything this big—going against his wishes. At some point we have to believe in ourselves.

Looking back over a lifetime of capitulation, it is not surprising that we blame ourselves; that is always the first line of recrimination. I believe I took no for an answer too meekly and gave up too easily and too often. But now, as women like me begin to build confidence and daring—and economic independence—we can reverse that pattern in our lives. We can, like Madeline, draw on the stubbornness and feistiness that come with this life stage to fight back and stand up for ourselves. A friend of mine proudly described an incident that made her feel she had finally—in her seventies—got it just right. A colleague and friend of hers had denounced her work publicly and viciously and then a couple of weeks later written her suggesting lunch as if nothing had happened. "I'm happy to say," my friend wrote back, "that I'm too old and too healthy to say yes."

We also draw on our inner "bitch" to help us zero in on what is worth fighting *for.* That isn't always immediately clear. Much of the work of Second Adulthood involves pruning away expectations, responsibilities, even people who no longer apply in order to get down to a core sense of what really matters. By becoming "outspoken, opinionated, and determined," we are developing the authority to reject outmoded priorities; then we can turn that authority to saying yes to new and meaningful ones.

Tichrahn sees her fifties as a symphony in forceful and empowering noes:

> *I say NO more than I ever have before. No to my children. No to family who try to infringe on my "personal alone just for me" time. I've paid my dues with men, married and divorced and have raised two great kids on my own. I date casually but when the gentleman tries to tell me how, or what or when, especially if it concerns my children, then they've stepped over the line of acceptable behavior. I voice my strengths and if they don't step back over the line onto their side, I walk away.*
>
> *. . . After seven years at a job where the male boss was verbally abusive and inconsiderate, I said no, not doing this anymore and quit over a month ago. Taking time for me and deciding a new direction. . . . We have found our voice.*

That voice is a little rusty—last heard from in full strength in childhood and muted, as psychologist Carol Gilligan has shown, at puberty. It is the voice of the terrible twos and the tyrannical teens. It is the voice that says "I want" and "I won't" with full-throated authority. For many of us it takes many false starts and lots of practice to literally clear our throat of the other more modulated voices that have usurped it over the intervening years: the rebellious-but-wheedling daughter voice; the firm-but-warm mother voice; the in-charge-but-cajoling wife voice; the competent-but-likable employee voice; and, in dealing with aging parents, the mother and daughter voices revived and combined. In the same way that running up and down the scales warms up an opera singer, saying no builds conviction, resonance, and often volume as well. Imagine if Jackie Kennedy Onassis, famous for her breathy manner of speaking, had found her no voice early on—she might have had as much impact on policy as she did on style.

Mary's husband calls her new voice "the schoolteacher." She is, in fact, a former school administrator who now teaches college and consults on conflict-mediation issues, but "the schoolteacher" emerged only in the last couple of years, in her midfifties. She remembers one incident in particular where she surprised and impressed herself:

> *Three years before I left the school system I went back from teaching to being a principal. In the school I went to there were two difficult parents—both mothers. They had a reputation for losing it and not being able to control themselves when they were upset. One in particular would*

lose it and yell at everyone and then go off into the parent room and have tea.

The teachers were stressed, people were acting as though they were walking on glass.

One day when she was doing that I just looked at her and said to myself this is not a mediation, this is not an arbitration. She should not be here.

I remember standing in the doorway of the parents' lounge and she was standing there with her daughter—she had pulled her out of class and wasn't allowing her to do the things I said she needed to do. I said, "Mrs. D. why isn't your daughter next door?" And she said, "She's not going anywhere, yah yah yah. . . ." I looked at her and the words just came out of my mouth. I said, "Well then I want you out of this building right now." She went. After she left other parents who had been sitting there brought me chocolate cookies.

She came back the next day as if nothing had happened. And her daughter did what I wanted. She put her back where I wanted.

I felt quite good about that at the time. Sometimes I think people who may be the boss look at people who did what I did and are at the point in their career or at the age I am and think, maybe she's getting to the point when she should retire. You want to look at them and say maybe it's just time we stood up a little more for what we're doing instead of just running around accommodating. What I did was important for the school, teachers, even important for her daughter.

I surprised myself that day. Ten years ago I would have

found any other possible way to do something different. I
used to stay quiet and go away and try to think of a way to
get around what I needed done.

While it is hard for most of us to find the courage to speak up
for the first time, some women have a particularly difficult time.
Physical abuse, to take the worst case, is frightening enough, but
fighting back is that much more frightening to a woman whose
self-worth has been eroded by a constant diet of noes from all
sides. Even a situation as simple as picking out a paint color can
be daunting to someone who has deferred to others for so long.
A decision as natural as choosing a kind of food to order in a
restaurant can stump a woman who has—to use Archie Bun-
ker's favorite shut-up verb for his wife Edith—"stifled" her right
to choose.

Even for less vulnerable women, the reactions to our first
defiant noes may be as dramatic as we fear. Intimates may feel
betrayed—"That isn't like you!" is a common charge. "It must
be menopause," is a common put-down. Family members may
see something worse: "You have gotten so *selfish*!" Others may
strike back with intimidating force and volume—not everyone
is as used to taking no for an answer as some of us used to be.
But we are ready. We have more resources available to us than
ever before. When the office manager, who has kept the machin-
ery running behind the scenes and soothed ruffled feathers
and hurt feelings for decades, says no to all that, she is breaking free. Even if she does not get the promotion or the raise she
is entitled to, even if she is accused of disloyalty, she will manage. When the women who make up the two-thirds of those
who initiate divorce in midlife stand up to power inequities in

their marriages, they know it will be hard, but they also know that they will make it. And if they don't know, their Horizontal Role Models will tell them. The women who have emerged from unsatisfactory marriages are some of the most energized I have spoken to.

Building up the nerve to say no to a destructive relationship is hard. Equally hard is overcoming the shock of discovery in a relationship that seemed fine. Disbelief can be as paralytic as fear. Robin, who is fifty-one and has a graphic design studio, had recently married the man she had been involved with for twenty-five years. She had moved into his apartment, but kept her own—which turned out to be fortuitous. Her "winter of discontent" began with a misdirected e-mail on her computer—and dragged on and on. Until she finally hatched her life-saving no.

> *I found out through an e-mail on my laptop, that he had picked up a woman—or she picked him up—it was just one of those whacko things: This was a girl that was 29 years old from Nebraska, and in forty-eight hours she's e-mailing him that she can't live without him—she's married, he's married, and it was like the person I knew, the person that I loved and adored, just turned on me, and turned before my eyes into this absolute unknown.*
>
> *When I confronted him, he basically said to me, "You really shouldn't look at my e-mails," and then within twenty-four hours she had sent naked photographs of herself. And then he was like, "Robin, it's just a chat room, you know I look at this stuff," and I'm like, "Okay." And what I did, which everybody thinks is so funny is that—you know*

for a moment you believe this stuff, you think, "well he can't be lying to me," and then you think, "wait a minute, that's so crazy." I said, "If this is what you're going to do and this is what's going on, go ahead, knock yourself out; I'm out of here." Then I got the tears, and "No, no, no," you know, "this is nothing," and for about two months I did that thing of holding on and believing and thinking it was all going to go away. But it just got worse and worse, and by the time—this was in November—by the time February rolled around, and I'd been put through the ringer with him, I didn't know what to do, and didn't know how much of what he was telling me was true and how much wasn't, I had never dealt with anything like this in my life. I only confided in one person, my Aunt Rita. I'd been around long enough to know that you don't talk about these kinds of things when you don't know what you're doing yourself. Because then you get everybody's opinion, or I do; I'm very influenced by people's opinion, and I really do care what people think, and I didn't want to be this woman that was letting this guy walk all over me, lie to me, and then I'm staying with him.

I had my own apartment, but I was in contact with him, and one day he came over, and I remember saying to him, you know, "If you're lying to me, and this is still going on, I just think that that would be unforgivable." And he looked at me, and he said, "I'm not lying." And he left, and I thought, "I'm never going to speak to that guy again." I just knew. *And I understand what they say in movies sometimes, when they say the person that you knew isn't there anymore. The person I know wasn't there anymore.*

Toxic relationships like Robin's can make us sick. Heartbreak and frustration put tremendous stress on the body. High levels of the stress hormone cortisol are a significant contributor to heart disease, and heart disease is the number one cause of death among women of all ages. A long-term British study of ten thousand government workers found that those who reported high levels of stress had a 68 percent higher risk of developing heart conditions than their less strung-out coworkers. Social scientists define an unhealthy job situation as a combination of too high demands and too little control over the work, and inadequate support from superiors and coworkers. The same toxicity measure—lots of pressure, little control, and less support—applies to most relationships we put it to. Saying no here can save your life.

Finding and saying yes to positive relationships and rewarding work environments can, on the other hand, literally keep us fit. The MacArthur Foundation Study of Aging in America found (as reported in Harvard Women's Health Watch) that "a job [paid or unpaid] that challenges your intellect, requires you to take initiative and make choices, and gives you confidence in your ability to handle a variety of situations can keep your mind sharp—much as physical workouts keep your body in shape."

Stress can also be self-generated, as we all know from years of rushing and multitasking and overcommitment. A woman named Kate wrote me, reporting an updated version of the hurry-up mode that she finds "the worst thing about being our age." It is the "feeling that you have to hurry. Hurry to do and raise a family, see to a husband, try to make a living. Hurry to figure out what everything is before your health fails. Hurry to be interesting and fun because you disappear more into the fabric of a younger society. Hurry to travel because the money won't go as far and we don't know how long it has to last. Hurry to become OK with yourself and your life and you have to be all right with that. Hurry and learn new technology they (younger people) talk about." Our capacity for making things hard for ourselves and setting ever-exalted expectations is infinite. It's a hard habit to break.

Supressed anger is an even more daunting form of internalized stress. In many situations, saying no lets some of that anger loose and takes some of the pressure off. But it is another of the ironies of this strange new world of ours that while our defiance is directed at seizing control of our lives, the anger that is behind it can make us feel just the opposite: out of control. Anger is a very delicate subject for most women. As Dr. Louann Brizendine explains in *The Female Brain,* we "have a much less direct relationship to anger" than men, both psychologically and neurologically. Pushing someone else too far, demanding too much, and escalating conflict are all situations that, for most of our lives so far, we would do almost anything to avoid.

The female brain is actually designed for conflict avoidance. It has a mechanism composed of "a series of circuits that hijack the emotion and chew on it, the same way a cow has an extra stomach that rechews its food before it is digested," explains Dr. Brizendine. Unless a woman is pushed over the edge—then there is no containing her response. But for the most part, a woman "will avoid anger or confrontation the same way a man will avoid an emotion," she concludes wryly.

Until now. Some of our newfound ferocity is, in fact, due to our revised hormonal profile. As estrogen levels drop, so does the level of oxytocin, a conflict-avoiding hormone. At the same time, the aggressive testosterone component becomes more influential. This recalibration results in a more balanced response system, but it also sets off a new reality in a woman's brain: a "take-no-prisoners view," as Dr. Brizendine puts it. She describes how this transformation manifested itself in a patient named Sylvia. As she "hit menopause, the filters came off, her irritability increased, and her anger wasn't headed for that extra 'stomach' anymore, to be chewed over before it came out. Her ratio of testosterone to estrogen was shifting, and her anger pathways were becoming more like a man's. The calming effects of progesterone and oxytocin weren't there to cool off the anger either." "This new brain cocktail," she concludes optimistically, "is a powerful stimulus for the road ahead."

Combined with the energy released by taking charge of our lives and the galvanizing commitment to what really matters, our anger is as powerful as we were afraid it would be—but also as empowering as we need it to be. "The anger of midlife is a ferocious anger," writes Erica Jong in *Fear of Fifty*. "In our twenties, with success and motherhood still before us, we could imagine that something would save us from second-classness— either achievement or marriage or motherhood. Now we know that nothing can save us. We have to save ourselves." Like many of the changes we are undergoing and precipitating, once the process is in motion, it is not at all clear where the chips will fall, but we are ready.

Some of those chips are downright delightful. The more we speak our minds, the more fun it can be. As I got deeper into my Fuck-You Fifties, I even found myself looking for opportunities to take on people I disagree with on issues I feel strongly about—just to prove to myself that I can do it. To prove that I am not "nice" anymore. And I must admit, to shock people.

The phrase itself has shock value—it does what it describes. When I use it, most women whoop with delight. As Peggy Northop, then the editor of *More* magazine, put it when I told her that it had once been suggested that I change the phrase to "the feisty fifties," "Nothing else quite captures the not-inconsiderable fear-bordering-on-thrill of what might happen when you carry this living-life-your-way—without apologies—to its logical conclusion. Will we get fired, or walk off the job? Will we become battle-axes, unfit for polite company? Will our marriages survive? 'Feisty' is way too tame for what this feels like!"

The "feisty fifties" suggestion confirms that there are still issues of "appropriate" behavior for women. Especially grown-up women. In the culture at large, as we become more and more "mature," "appropriate" seems to verge on "invisible."

In our ongoing battle with roles and rules, one of the most no-intensive obstacles is the bitter message that our last role is invisibility. A major AARP survey of women over forty-five asked respondents to answer the question "Which have you personally experienced because of your age?" They were offered three areas of negative treatment:

Job related (not hired, not advanced, fired)
Consumer related (ignored or patronized)
Socially related (excluded or disregarded)

Despite the acknowledged pervasiveness of workplace discrimination, twice as many women in the survey reported experiencing consumer and social invisibility.

We are all familiar with the salesperson who points across the store rather than accompanies you to the merchandise, and with the maitre d' who automatically seats older women diners in the farthest—and darkest—reaches of the restaurant. I find it especially hard to accept that some younger person with whom I am trying to make conversation is looking for the earliest opportunity to get away.

As our lives become more noteworthy, interesting, and out-there, we are less likely to fade into the woodwork. The consumer industry is awakening to our buying power at the same time as our no voice is rising against marketing that is insulting or irrelevant to our lives. The media are beginning to feature some of the older women who, by dint of talent and beauty as well as power, won't go away. Accomplished women in every profession are being recognized, even as they accumulate birthdays alongside the men. But it is incumbent on us, as the pioneer generation, to keep pushing back against being dismissed unceremoniously whenever it happens.

The Red Hat Society, founded in 1998, has become a worldwide network of women over fifty who are saying no to all that in word and deed. Its close to a million members pride themselves on being outrageous; they wear eye-catching red hats and go on field trips and luncheons en masse. "We just enjoy going out to public places once a month and letting everyone know we can dress how we want and don't care what anyone else thinks about it," says founder Sue Ellen Cooper, otherwise known as the Exalted Queen Mother. "We always make heads turn in our regalia," says a happy member. "It is obvious we are out to have a good time." The organization also has a commendable mission: "to gain higher visibility for women in our age group and to reshape the way we are viewed by today's culture."

Members of one Red Hat chapter refer to themselves as "the

hot and spicy ladyz" in an effort to rename the life experience they are celebrating. Back in the seventies, when what we were doing was called Women's Lib, it became clear that in order to participate in the conversation about what we were up to, it was essential to gain control over the vocabulary that applied to us. Saying no to the honorifics *Miss* and *Mrs.*, which defined a woman by her marital status, was a defiant act. At first, the use of *Ms.* was ridiculed as a title for a "half-man woman." The term finally made its way into the language as an accepted form of address for any adult female. That simple but potent clerical change restored our privacy and enhanced our independence. As we outgrow the age-bound descriptives—*old, older, oldest*— we are going to need a comparably defining moniker for our cohort. We can certainly do better than *boomer* or *hot and spicy ladyz* or, worst of all, *senior.* I personally hate *crone* and *elder.* The Transition Network organized a name-our-generation contest. The winner was *the REgeneration.* This search for the right words is not about semantics; it is about self-definition.

As we build a new stage of life in word—however impolite— and deed—however "inappropriate"—we are changing the conversation among and within women. When a woman announces with amazed discovery, "I don't care what people think anymore!" what she really means is—as poet Robin Morgan puts it—"I *do* care what people think, but I care more what *I* think!" Every time one of us exercises her right to say no, she is building the know-how and self-knowledge to say yes, with conviction.

For me, the nurturing nature of no is becoming more encompassing with practice. My Fuck-You Fifties are giving way to my Sez-Me Sixties. I hadn't registered this shift until the day I spent the morning canceling and rescheduling appointments. It suddenly dawned on me that in the course of inventing the rest of my life, I had stopped feeling compelled to show up where I was supposed to, simply because I was supposed to; I was learning to ask myself: "So, do you want to do that, do you need to do that—yes or no?"

For years I cherished a fantasy gift: one canceled lunch per month. When someone else couldn't make an appointment, I was grateful; it didn't occur to me that I could give myself the gift of needed time to attend to other priorities. I always showed up. I remember once traveling an hour to spend a few minutes speaking to a journalism class when I was almost delirious with fever. Another time I showed up for an exam the day I had received some truly traumatic news—even though I knew plenty of people who regularly got a medical excuse from exams due to cramps! (I flunked, by the way.) Countless times a week I shortchanged myself (skipped the trip to the ladies' room, postponed the makeup renewal, didn't pause to catch my breath) in order to show up—and on time.

No more! I now delight in the ease with which appointments can be moved around and requests turned down without throwing the planet off its orbit. Which is not to say that I am careless with my commitments. Everyone who matters to me can count on me—even more so now that I am getting good at prioritizing my time. Now that I am in the swing of it, I relish the moment when I hear myself tell myself, "No, I don't think I can get to that." I am especially pleased when the true reason is simply that I don't feel like it. Sez who? Sez me!

Decisions about showing up have taken on a new meaning for me; each one is a way of saying yes to being present for my own life, and saying no to fulfilling an expectation in someone else's. I hear that same sense of fresh air in a note from Mary Louise: "Fifteen years ago (is that possible?) I met and started dating a man," she writes, "and we have been dating ever since!!! No marriage, just dating. . . . 'Once was enough,' we both say, and as surely as fish swim in the water, if we got married it would last about three months, if that long!!! It's something about having one's own space and being in control of it and one's own life without having to answer to anyone."

Some time around her fiftieth birthday, Anne found herself embarking on what turned out to be a major yes/no learning curve. At the time she was into a happy third marriage, enjoying her stepchildren, and deeply committed to her career in progressive politics. "From like '68 to '94," she recalls, "it's like I'm always pushing myself . . . I couldn't rest until I figured out how to help change society so that utter injustice couldn't continue."

The problem was that no matter how happy her circumstances appeared or effective she looked—and was—she didn't *feel* empowered to call the shots in her own life. "It was like I was depleted," she says of that turning point ten years ago. "I was like 'Okay, I've learned enough; I've pushed myself into a lot of situations, but personally I had gotten into a very narrow life.'" She slowly began to take stock; she quit her paid political job and devoted herself to a not-for-profit activist organization. But that didn't seem to make any difference; she was still "pushing" herself to keep up with her responsibilities.

The crisis came when her brother's chronic blood disorder took a turn for the worse the same week when she was in the midst of planning an important board retreat. When she got the news, she found herself torn between showing up for work and showing up for family. With her husband's encouragement she said no to the retreat and yes to her heart. Her brother died three days later. Making that choice, obvious as it might have been to someone else, was a major catalyst for her. "There is a line in *Death of a Salesman*," she says, looking back, "where Willie Loman's wife says, 'Attention must be paid, attention must be paid.' It was clear to me that there are certain times in you life when *attention must be paid*. I was in another dimension."

While mourning her brother's death, she contemplated her own life; she realized that despite all the adjustments that had taken place in the past several years, she hadn't really changed her core priorities. She was finally ready to do that: to issue some important yeses and noes. The most precious element in her life, she concluded, was "this adorable man who's bright and funny and smart and I feel great when I'm with him," his children, and the grandchildren. "This marriage has just gotten better and better, and I don't know when I'm going to die; I don't how or when he is going to die," she muses. "But when I get overly responsible or I get fixed on something, I get very preoccupied and I'm not present for him." She asked herself two questions: "Why don't I take advantage of this man who loves me and wants nothing else but me?" and "What the fuck am I doing with this crazy board that just spins themselves around these things that they think are so goddam important?" The answers became clear only after, as she puts it, "I gave myself permission to put myself first."

The first yes/no move was to focus on her marriage and pull back from the demands of her work, quitting the most stressful board and cutting back the hours she spent on the phone with work-related follow-ups from home. She felt good about that yes to her personal life, but the more she pared away at the excesses of her work life, the clearer it became that the component of social activism in her life was *not* dispensable. It was another definite *yes*! Along with her important relationships, that passion was authentic. With that clarity, she began to find ways to get her priorities in sync. "I still have my 'to do' list, but I feel like I'm clear, like I'm putting it out there and if people like it, if it goes well, if it accomplishes what I hope, fine; but I'm not that worried about it any more; I'm not trying so hard, it's just like if it's going to happen it's going to happen. . . ." What has changed? "I have learned that I need to renew myself, that I need to let myself off the hook."

I could hear the relief in her voice as she summed up her new outlook, and I pictured a more low-key chapter ahead for her. That was not the way she saw it at all. She was joining another board, she announced to me, one with an international reach, a more demanding schedule, and more intense mission than the one she had liberated herself from not so long ago. I was having trouble seeing the difference between her pre-no self and her post-no self. Why on earth was she putting herself back into the kind of stressful situation that had shortchanged her internal life? Because, she explained, there was a difference in her attitude. "I'm going to manage how to use myself," she said. "I'm going to make sure I ask myself: How can I enjoy it? What's the part of it that I can be a part of and still be present for my husband and still be present to my own needs? I'll have to do it differently, that's the challenge."

I finally understood that although the objective elements in her life hadn't changed as much as many women's do when they start saying no, the way she perceived those elements and the way she dealt with them was as radical as moving from the tropics to the North Pole. "The thing that upsets people is not what happens," the Greek philosopher Epictetus wrote, "but what they think it means." Anne was no longer upset by the pressures of her work, because she had rejected both extraneous and self-imposed demands. Her emotional connections were thriving, because she had accepted and was reveling in the fact that that was where her deepest commitment was. Her priorities were in order.

Second Adulthood women are learning the uses of a well-placed no. It is another of the resources that come to the surface as we navigate new waters. For us, saying no, is not about simply giving the finger to the world; it is about assertiveness, affirmation, and self-definition. For Anne, no had become yes as a result of her unique and authentic internal recalibration. It doesn't matter how it looks from the outside. In fact, that is the whole point.

Building a life of one's own, one no and one yes at a time, is what we mean by the goal I hear articulated again and again: authenticity. We want to find our true path and follow it. We want to be honest and forthright with our friends. We want to draw loving limits within our families. We want to do our best work in the world. Each and every one of those objectives requires the courage of each woman's convictions: what she rejects and what she affirms.

THE LESSON: Saying no is the password into your new life. It isn't as easy as it may look, but with every assertion of independence, with every rejection of unwanted demands, and with every act of standing up to insult or authority, you get stronger. And begin to have more fun. At some moments you may become overwhelmed by anger as you realize how long you have put up with things you wanted to say no to. You may not be able to figure out right away what you want to do next. But when your voice has gotten strong enough, you will know that when you say yes you really mean it.

Lesson Four

A "Circle of Trust" Is a Must

Time passes.

Life happens. Distance separates.

Children grow up.

Jobs come and go.

Love waxes and wanes.

Men don't do what they're supposed to do.

Hearts break.

Parents die.

Colleagues forget favors.

Careers end.

BUT . . .

Sisters are there, no matter how much time and how many miles are between you. A girlfriend is never farther away than needing her can reach.

—Circulated on the Internet

I hate sappy Hallmark-card poetry, and when it shows up in my e-mail, I generally delete it unopened. So do most of my friends—the very ones who have been sending me the treacly lines above for years, always with the tagline "This one is worth reading." They just can't help themselves. When it comes to close friends, the most steely of us becomes sentimental. Even my college-age daughter, who never passes on inspirational messages, forwarded the version that was circulating among her sorority sisters. Each woman who passed it along did so because she felt that, unlike other subjects of purple prose, friendship among women is worthy of it, and the message in the setup to the "sisters" e-mail from the unknown Horizontal Role Model is so important:

> *I sat drinking iced tea and visiting with my mother, when she said, "Don't ever forget your girlfriends, because no matter how much you love your husband, you are still going to need your girlfriends. Remember to go places with them now and again, even if you don't want to. And remember that girlfriends include sisters, mothers, daughters, grandmothers, not just friends—women supporting and relating to other women is our gift and our responsibility to each other."*
>
> *What a strange bit of advice, I thought, [back when] I was newly married and not some young girl who needed her friends. I did listen though, and stayed in touch with my girlfriends and found new friends along the way. And as the years tumbled by, I came to fully understand that Mom really knew what she was talking about!*

It's rare for a daughter to admit that mother knows best, but this is clearly so fundamental a Life Lesson that it is moving from one generation to the next with real conviction and urgency. That my daughter thought to pass along the affirmation of women's friendship is her way of saying to me that she believes in it as much as she knows I do. She would be surprised to hear that I didn't always feel that way.

What she takes for granted about friendship, I had to learn much later in life. She would never treat a social commitment to a girlfriend as a stopgap until a better (preferably male) offer comes along, as was standard operating procedure in my time. She often chooses the company of her friends over other offers. They have spats and disappointments that are momentarily the end of the world, but best friends are not the untrustworthy secret rivals I grew up fearing they were. Even playground games we played—jump rope, hopscotch, tag—pitted us against one another rather than called for teamwork; and the low stakes of those games reinforced a cultural attitude toward competitive girls: that their lack of feminine modesty would alienate other girls and their tomboyishness would alienate boys. In such a climate, any desire to win was driven underground. We acquired manipulative and coy tricks, which included betraying one another, to get us what we wanted by more devious means than simply going for it. We have had to unlearn all that.

My generation came to trust our women friends when we were in our twenties and thirties as we took the risk of articulating experiences that were humiliating and exclusionary and intimidating. We got angry together and then began to take action together and rejoice in our triumphs in the struggle for equality—in the workplace, in politics, in the home—together. As young mothers, we learned to count on the advice and reassurance of those who were exploring the nature of motherhood alongside us. And now as we age, we are counting more than ever on our compadres to move through this bewildering and challenging life stage with us, as a team.

Recognizing the importance of our friendships is part of a recalibration of What Matters to us now. Myrna, one of the most unsentimental and confident women I know, recently admitted that she felt lost after the death of a dear friend. "We were supposed to grow old together," she lamented. Indeed, growing older with friends gives us a context for our own aging. At least as much as our life partners, our close friends are the ones we are really pledged to stick by "for better and for worse, for richer and poorer, in sickness and in health." Perhaps that is why when women my age talk about a precious "circle of trust," we do so with wonder and reverence. Maybe we send one another schmaltzy poetry to express those feelings.

Ethel reached a crossroads with her friendships when she was in her late forties. She had been a very successful academic, brought a sexual harassment suit against a fellow professor and (coincidentally?) lost her teaching post; she got active in politics and started her own consulting business. Traveling became a way of life for her and although she could name many intimate friends, she didn't see them as often as she needed to. That began to bother her, especially when she decided to stop looking for the right man and "move forward." She turned "inward to kind of figure out what was important to me. I'd had this successful career and then I had this business, but what did I really want to do? I really wanted to reestablish a community."

The friends she wanted to get back to were not waiting for her. "The community that I created earlier was changing; my friends who had been single for a long time started getting married, and you know when you get married, you kind of go and be with that person for a while and then you reemerge. And I had friends move away. So," she admits. "I found myself increasingly lonely, which had never been an issue for me before."

She realized she had some reconstructing to do. "When I was younger I was very self-involved; I traveled a lot, and I just assumed everybody would understand I was gone, and then I'd come back. But," she discovered, sooner or later, "people just say, our lives have gone on, we have a full life here and sure you can drop by, but it's not the same thing as being part of people's lives. So part of it was really getting back to good friends and having to deal with some of their annoyances that I was gone."

An unintended consequence of renewing those relationships was getting involved with the children who had appeared on the scene while she was AWOL. "Children require you to be present," she learned. "They don't really care how important you think you were or are; they don't really care what you did yesterday, it's really about what are you doing with me today? And being present was not one of my strong suits. . . . I love these kids; you play with them and suddenly you can see the world in a new way. They really changed my life." But, she adds, "I had a three-hour rule; I was like the best playmate for three hours, and then that was it."

As she worked on her old friendships, Ethel became aware of other ways that friends were important to her new outlook on the rest of her life. "I needed some new friends just to feel like my life was new. You know meeting new people is a way to make you feel like you're young; there's new learning, there's new excitement, and I needed to be in a slightly different world. So I made new friends, and my new friends were not as professionally successful—their lives were more about their communities and friends and going to basketball games, women's basketball games, and having picnics, and so it helped put some balance in my life."

Most of the friends I cherish are from school (one, with whom I have rebonded after thirty years, was my best friend in third grade) or work (the foursome with whom I have had dinner every month since 1989) or children (the dear, experienced mother of three who reassured me that, yes, I could rub a little scotch on those tender gums). But as we change our lives, our needs shift, and those friends who may have been experts in one experience are less so in others. Since they, too, are changing their lives, our interests may be diverging.

One friend, a relatively new one at that, admits that she has consciously changed all her important friends in the last ten years. She actively cultivates women whose work she admires and who seem to be deeply committed to making things happen; they keep her on her toes, which is where she wants to be for the rest of her life.

But I am becoming increasingly aware that many women do not have enough access to one another. For one thing, opportunities to make new friends are harder to come by. One woman I know who is working from home in a new community saw a woman in a yoga class who looked interesting. "I didn't know how to approach her, though," she said. "It was sort of like asking someone out on a first date." A series of incidents focused my attention on the longing that many women feel for connection with other women who are in the same boat:

On a spring morning not long ago therapists Karen Van Allen and Ruth Neubauer and I led a workshop on the transition into Second Adulthood. We met in a community center in the suburbs of Washington, D.C., and had a wonderful time laughing about our shared predicament, delighting in the discovery that none of us was alone—or crazy—and supporting one another in facing the tough decisions described to the group. I had expected this kind of spontaneous bonding to emerge in that setting, but what I hadn't expected was more sobering. I was struck by how much of what these women were dealing with had to do with how isolated they felt living in scattered enclaves around a high-power city, and how rejected they felt by the workplace community, where everyone was younger and more ambitious than they were.

The most concrete outcome of that workshop was a commitment the group made to a regular potluck supper. "It was amazing to all of us," Jeanne wrote me after their first meeting, "how easily we picked up from 45 days prior when we all sat together that Sunday. The conversation was comfortable and again for me reassuring and empowering. Several of us mentioned after the fact that we had our doubts about whether the connection would still be there, but it most definitely was. And," she added, "the food was delicious." As they move forward, the group plans to read books and go out together, and they hope that little by little they will become invested in one another.

Another event that caught my attention was the response to the glorious Dove "pro-aging" ad campaign launched in early 2007. We all loved the images of exuberant, proud, and totally beautiful women photographed in all their nude and gravity-challenged glory. I am sure many women rushed out, as I did, to buy their products in order to support the company's support of us. And many rushed to the Dove Web site to register their delight and gratitude. But once there, those women didn't want to leave—they posted long, passionate, confessional entries about how they felt about their bodies and about being women in an ageist culture. They wrote like girlfriends. And they wrote like women who didn't have enough real-life girlfriends to share their lives with. I doubt that the Dove folks anticipated creating such a dynamic and meaningful community.

The third event that expanded my awareness of the problem was a visit with a cousin I don't see very often. She had very nice things to say about my writing, but she took issue with my wholehearted and unrelenting celebration of a "circle of trust" in the lives of women. Her experience has been different, she told me. She has never trusted women and still doesn't. "If anything, I trust men more," she said. This despite the fact that her first husband betrayed her big-time. The lesson she took from that and some other disappointments in her life is that women can't be trusted not to try to steal your man. And they can't be trusted to wish you well. Still, she longs for a circle she could feel differently about, but her efforts to find one haven't panned out yet. When she went to a meeting of a group that sews for a charity gift shop, she was dismayed by the tone of the conversation and not surprised to find that the group's nickname is "stitch and bitch." She is still looking for a more welcoming and generous circle.

Other women I have talked to since have had similar experiences. "I find that my tolerance for 'fluff' or gossip has almost vanished. I don't care what actress is doing what with whom. . . ." one told me. "As I've gotten older," she explains, "I care less about what other people are doing, unless it affects me personally. I don't care how much my coworkers make or what vehicles they drive. I've come to think more about the larger picture. I've become more involved with certain political issues. I've taken some classes and read some books relating to Buddhism, and this philosophy really seems to make sense to me." But she has yet to find a compatible circle of friends.

All of these women would welcome a scheme that Gloria Steinem envisions: a network of AA-style "leaderless meetings" in every town and city, where a newcomer or someone looking for more empathic input into her life could just show up. The schedule and locations would appear in local newspapers and the confidentiality of the conversation would be inviolate. A literal "circle of trust." You could check in for a shot in the arm of woman talk or you could become a regular. Weight Watcher meetings are probably as close as we get right now.

Conversations about unsatisfactory friendships have made me reconsider my assumptions. I had been writing from a perspective that assumed our generation had outgrown that wariness of other women. I had also assumed that readers would understand that not every woman was a potential "sister." I realized that I, too, could point to some disappointing experiences. The "new friend" I invited to my sixty-fifth birthday party hasn't been heard from. And the pain from a friendship that fell apart twenty years ago is still alive. She and her husband were probably our closest friends. We spent weekends together, more remarkable for the fact that they had children and we hadn't yet. She helped me get a job I loved, where she worked.

Ultimately I was in a position where I had a say in her salary and the amount of recognition her work received, but after a couple of years, due to a series of misunderstandings and some incomplete information, she came to believe that I was not looking out for her. A blowup of gigantic proportions left both of us scarred and estranged. Sad.

How, then, do you find opportunities to connect, and how do you make good choices about new friends? Studies have shown, for example, that one of the primary reasons women go back to school, in addition to wanting to expand their horizons or update their skills, is to meet other women. Book clubs are another gathering place; by choosing books about women's experience, many seem to function as modern-day consciousness-raising groups. Looking up old friends who have drifted off has brought surprising rewards for some. I am hearing wonderful stories about stretch classes that turned into support groups, investment clubs that changed the lives of the members, and—one of my favorites—what happened when thirteen strangers—all in their fifties—banded together to buy a diamond necklace.

I read about Jewelia, as the necklace was lovingly called, in *People* magazine a couple of years ago. It seems that one woman fell in love with it and kept returning to the jewelry store to try it on. After several of those visits, the owner suggested that she get a group together to buy the necklace and, he added, "I'll drop the price if my wife could join the group." So she did just that: she assembled a dozen women who barely knew one another but liked the outrageousness of the scheme. The plan was that the necklace would change hands at a regular monthly meeting. There were only two rules: you had to wear it at least once while making love, and anyone who went to Paris got to take it along.

Well, you can imagine what happened. Over the years, as the women got to know each other and enjoy their extravagant adventure, the monthly meetings became more precious than the necklace they were set up to pass along. For the bookkeeper whose sister had just died, the group enabled her to "reconnect with life again"; the self-described "biker chick" couldn't believe that thirteen women could "share such a gorgeous piece of jewelry and not fight over it"; a member who was going through a divorce felt the group's support "through one of the most difficult times in my entire life"; and the "earth mother type" has "moral issues about Jewelia" but cherishes the "warmth of the women."

We can't expect to find more than one or two new best friends. The intimacy is so sensitive, the chemistry so subtle. Obviously, we have to have experiences and interests in common and a willingness to share our stories, but the most important ingredient, the one that builds a precious trust between us, is *how* we share our stories. How we listen. When we ask. How we attend to one another. How we laugh. That is why each new friend—and every old friend—is a gift.

Another anonymous Internet posting (diabetics beware!) puts it this way:

Girlfriends keep your children and your secrets.
Girlfriends don't always tell you you're right, but they usually tell you the truth.
Girlfriends still love you even if they disagree with your choices.

Girlfriends listen when you lose a job or a friend.
Girlfriends listen when your children break your heart.
Girlfriends listen when your parents' minds and bodies fail.

Tim Madigan's lovely book, *I'm Proud of You: My Friendship with Fred Rogers,* captures the unique gifts of TV's Mr. Rogers, who was a one-man circle of trust. When I met Fred back in the 1980s, I marveled at how children thronged to him wherever he went; they were frequently joined by their mothers, who had the same soft expression on their faces as the children. I asked him about those mothers, and he told me that again and again one would whisper to him that she watched his show along with her kids, because his mantra—"I like you just the way you are"— offered the simple friendlike acceptance she needed. Rogers understood the universal longing for tender validation. A letter he wrote Madigan recounts his delight at discovering "the South African word *ubuntu,* which means: 'I am because we are.' 'Isn't that lovely!' he said. 'My identity is such that includes you. I would be a very different person without you.'"

Given all the evidence of the nurturing nature of friendship, it is alarming to hear that Americans seem to be moving in smaller and smaller circles of friends. The *American Sociological Review* reported a "remarkable drop" in the size of people's "core network of confidants." In 1985 the average American had three close friends; by 2004 it was down to two. And those with none jumped from 10 percent to 25 percent. Such statistics are probably due to many variables, including increased work hours and less time to relate to others, geographical distance, long commutes, and technology—we hook up with machines more often than with friends. And such statistics certainly apply more to men than to women; the rampant sense of isolation and despair reported by men in our age group is becoming a major health concern. But the overall message of this study is that not only are we right to cherish our friendships but we will also have to accept that it may be harder than ever to cultivate new ones.

Here is how some of the Horizontal Role Models I have talked to are experiencing friendship in the context of their changing lives:

MARGE: *What does your circle of trust look like? Is it made up of women with the same interests as you? So, maybe you have interlocking circles of trust. For example, I am building a circle of women writers. I have another circle that all live in my community. A couple of women are in both circles, so the circles interlink. The writing circle has been forming (slowly) over the last three years. Not everyone that "has always wanted to write" is ready to be in a writing group. When you share writing, you are opening your soul and sharing your vision. For the circle to be a safe place to share on such an intimate level, there has to be a generosity of spirit and trustworthiness in each person.*

CAROLE: *Frequently lapsed friendships are due to different life paths at different times; however, those same friendships pick right up again where they left off as our life paths converge again at future points. This too is an inspiring and amazing turn of events in our lives.*

KATE: *I have gone from thinking I would be one of the Married-with-secure-life-style type of woman to a totally unknown Figure-it-out-as-you-go single. My WASband [get it?] of 28 years told me he was not having a "midlife crisis" he was having a "midlife AWARENESS." Well that awareness turned out to be named Vicki. Old story . . . new life . . . for me. That has begun quite a path to a new and different awareness . . . of myself as a person; as a dating single; as a divorced mother with grown children who have questioned and decided to blame; to deciding what it truly means to reinvent your life.*

I started dating, went into a serious four-year relationship, followed my intuition and left that. I am 55 and it is time to breathe deeply and fully . . . and learn to do that on a daily basis.

One of the difficult things for me is the fact that although I have a wonderful loving caring circle of friends, they are all married. At my age it is difficult to find women who are single that are on the irreverent edge of life. There is SO much to go and do . . . and laugh about . . . and have a "fuck it" attitude one day, yet be available to walk the traditional path other days.

AUDREY: *Here comes the next stage in the rich tapestry of life. We have lost so many of our family and friends over the past few years, and each time a friend dies, it is so much of your own life's memories that die with them. It seems to me that part of mourning erodes one's own identity. . . . Conversely this also has a dramatic effect. You say to yourself: I am still alive; I should not waste this life I have—which is a good sense to have.*

MARY: *I seek out women for different reasons. I used to have friends from the workplace and we were just friends because we had a common bond through work. I do not see them anymore. I am not in touch with any of my childhood friends or any of my college roommates. I have a friend that I like to see as she challenges my way of thinking about books, politics, and the world at large, which my closest friend does not. I have three young friends that I see every couple of months and we share what is going on in the world and in what is now their world of work. I feel sometimes as if I am their mother and at other times their mentor. Another group of retired educators who consider themselves my friends and I theirs ask me to go to lunch with a group of teachers I know, but I really do not want to spend time with this group. It does give me pause at times as I wonder how I will fare as an old lady with few friends and maybe being left on my own as I have been so choosy about who I spend time with now. I cannot believe that I should choose more friends to avoid being lonely in my old age—but the thought does cross my mind.*

MAREE: *I am a strong introvert and so not inclined to great revelation at the deepest level except with a VERY special friend. My VERY special friend died a year and a half ago and I miss her hugely. She was that amazing being to whom I could tell anything. She was my soul friend. So now I journal a lot and seek her wisdom from wherever she is.*

One level up from that DEEP PLACE I have half a dozen very strong friends with whom I would share a lot. Criteria for such friendship would include:

  —mutuality of sharing and revealing

  —a common value base (ethics, politics—small p)

  —the other woman also being on a journey, and conscious of that

  —being psychologically reasonably intact—I have found it too draining to have to support people if they won't seek professional support when they need it—selfish perhaps but honest.

Honest indeed, and as good a check list as I have found.

Maree and Audrey and the rest are instinctively confirming what scientists are reporting—that friends are good for body and soul. Friendship among women is one of the most dynamic topics in the field of gender behavior. Melissa Healy, a reporter for the *Los Angeles Times*, has captured the spirit of the relationship and also assembled studies that demystify many aspects of its chemistry:

Women are keepers of each other's secrets, boosters of one another's wavering confidence, co-conspirators in life's adventures. Through laughter, tears and an inexhaustible river of talk, they keep each other well, and make each other better.

Across species and throughout human cultures, females have banded together for protection and mutual support. They have groomed each other, tended each other's young, nursed each other in illness and engaged in the kind of aimless sociability that has generally mystified male anthropologists.

But the power of girlfriends is beginning to yield its secrets to science. For women, friendship not only rules, it protects. It buffers the hardships of life's transitions, it lowers blood pressure, boosts immunity and promotes healing. It may help explain one of medical science's most enduring mysteries: why women, on average, have lower rates of heart disease and longer life expectancies than men.

Shelley E. Taylor, a social neuroscientist at the University of California, Los Angeles, has studied how men and women deal with one of life's most persistent assaults—stress—and why women in groups cope better. It used to be thought that all human animals responded to external threats by a rush of adrenaline in what was accepted as the fight-or-flight response. But one particularly stressful day in their lab, Taylor and her female colleagues noticed something very interesting: the stressed-out men stormed into their offices and slammed the doors, while the women came *out* of their offices and started making coffee together. This anecdotal insight led to research that concluded that women have a "tend and befriend" instinct when threatened; they gather with other women and work to solve the problem and defuse the tension. The stress-reducing nature of women's support of one another is one possible explanation of why women are living longer than men.

Other studies have looked into the hormonal mechanism behind the calming factor. It turns out that when women are working together, or simply enjoying one another's company, oxytocin is released. Often referred to as "the cuddle hormone," it is most commonly associated with breast-feeding, but, Taylor explains, "We call it a 'social thermostat' that keeps track of how well (females') social supports are going." When the thermostat reads too low, females tend to reach out to others. When they reach out to others, oxytocin levels rise again and with that prolonged exposure comes a distinctive "calming, warm" effect. As a result, stress is less likely to do the kind of physiological damage that can lead to chronic diseases such as heart disease and metabolic disorders. At the same time, high levels of oxytocin and reliable social support networks seem to boost the immune system. "We don't see the same mechanisms in men," Taylor adds.

Healy's reporting found several studies suggesting "that the broader network of friends and support that women tend to have may also protect then from the effects of dementia." A Swedish survey concluded that the risk of developing dementia was lowest in men and women who maintained a wide variety of satisfying contacts with friends and relatives. "The researchers surmised that the mental exercise of juggling many relationships kept the brains of those with rich social networks in better tone."

Finally, Healy turned up proof of something that we have suspected all along—when everything is going wrong, a man can't "make it better" the way a woman can. We aren't making this up. "German researchers found that when subjects were given a stressful task—in this case, preparing a speech for delivery in front of an audience—men who were joined by their female partner for the preparation period showed much lower stress levels than those who had no support. For women, it was a different story. When women preparing their speeches were joined by their male partners, their stress hormones surged."

I know from experience with my own women's network and with my well-meaning but take-charge husband that sharing a problem elicits very different vibes. The women mobilize around a reassuring we-can-work-together-on-this message. My husband's first response is usually a defensive "what do you expect me to do about it?" When I assure him I have no superhero expectations of him, that I only want his advice, he relaxes a bit, only to try to help by interrogating me about the choices and decisions that created the crisis. He thinks he is getting to the root of the problem; I feel on trial.

"Men's support to a friend or partner tends to take the form of advice," neuroscientist Taylor says. "Women's support more frequently comes in vaguer forms of encouragement, validation and acceptance. That, in turn, may let a woman work out her own solution to a problem, with less pressure to satisfy the expectations of her adviser. This insight may explain why a married man is more likely to live longer than a single one, because of the companionship of the woman he is married to. A married woman, though, does not do so well, if she doesn't also have a circle of friends."

The friends and coauthors of *This Is Not the Life I Ordered* offer a nice way of thinking about the empowering nature of women's intimacy. "Many think of courage . . . as a solitary journey. We believe the journey of courage is best walked with women friends who literally and figuratively 'en-courage' us."

Here is a story of how one new friendship grew. The fact that it reads almost like a love story underlines the combination of fear and longing that accompanies the risk of opening up to a new person—a friend as much as a lover—and the rewards.

Annie is fifty-three "and a half." She is married for the second time and though the marriage is "unphysical (my choice)," it is "okayish. We get along." She has a teenage daughter who delights her, and a growing interest in an alternative school of

psychology called Reiki, a Japanese technique for stress reduc-
tion, relaxation, and healing by enhancing and guiding one's
"life-force energy."

*I have never had many friends, as I have moved many
times in my life. However in the last three years the deep
need, almost painfully so, to connect with women has been
immense. I listen to others having conversations about people they know, and I'm puzzled as to how they can know
some of the things they do from so far back. I lost my childhood friends over and over, until I stopped making them. It
has made it tricky creating new friendships, to say the least.
So how did this one begin? With a blueberry. Yep, with
a blueberry. I was going through the check-out in a local
store last summer, when blueberries were in season, and a
reasonable price. The woman on the check-out said she'd
never had one before, so I took one out and gave it to her.
She set it aside, but I told her she'd forget it if she didn't eat
it now, so she did, and enjoyed it too.*

*After that I would go through Angela's check-out and
we would chat and then one day she asked me if I'd been
the one who'd given here the blueberry. When I said, yes,
we laughed about it and thus began conversations that
were a little more involved than just hi, how are you. We
shared names and some more personal information. Angela
told me about an out of body experience she had years ago,
and of the impact it has had on her. I talked about Reiki
and some of the things I was reading about, and Angela
showed a lot of interest. I would run ideas by her and she'd
give me her opinion.*

Not long ago, I was contacted by someone about teaching Reiki as a 40th birthday present for someone I'd met at a workshop. I was interested in doing a new training, and thought I'd earn the money to pay for it by teaching Reiki. I shared all this with Angela, who was as excited as I was.

It all dragged on; I went away for a week, then they had school holidays, then I was being my daughter's coach in the psych and nutrition department for the London Marathon, and then this proud mother watched her daughter come in on tv! . . . All of this I shared with Angela, whose own daughter is a few months older than mine, and the bond became stronger. Then about May, Angela asked me if I would explain to her more about Reiki and we agreed to get together for a day. I guess that is when we went from two women who had lots to talk about and were friendly to becoming really good friends. We sat in her kitchen after lunch and chatted for a while; then Angela suggested that we have a cup of tea and sit in more comfortable chairs. When we went through [to the living room] I looked at the clock and it said 4:30!!! Time had simply vanished in our conversation!!

We shared our stories, laughed, explored, and discovered we really liked each other tremendously. Like me, Angela has had few women friends in her life. She's 61, though she doesn't look it!, and living with her daughter after her divorce, which she instigated (those statistics again!). Her desire to develop her spiritual life has gone largely unanswered until now. So when an idea I had for starting a Reiki school began to develop, grow wings and start to fly, she was right there beside me. I am not sure what it was *that took us from one point to the next, but it happened within the time frame of the five hours we spent together talking that day . . .*

The tentative first steps of friendship involve such a delicate balance of risks and payoffs that it is no wonder we fear the commitment and long for it at the same time. It takes courage—and encouragement. Even established friendships benefit from the increased attention we are inclined to give them now. We are building more profound connections. For one thing, we are increasingly drawn to the "big issues" and the deeper questions. We simply don't mess around. And we don't waste time on social frills. The Fuck-You Fifties free us from anxiety about appearing foolish, on the one hand, and fitting in, on the other. "It matters less that others agree with me than it matters that I choose," writes Hawaiian writer and teacher Yvonne Mokihana Calizar in an essay entitled "Nana I Ke Ku . . . Looking to the Source." Because we are so invested in making our own choices at last, it really means something that we call our dearest friends our "*chosen* family."

THE LESSON: Friendship is the sine qua non for whatever is going to work for us as we explore the rest of our lives. Old friends ground us, connect our past to our future, and tell us the truth. New friends expand our horizons and challenge us to be authentic in a relationship right from the start. The companionship of like-minded women gives us courage, reduces stress, and is the best problem-solving environment there is. And the laughter we generate together is, as we all know, the elixir of life.

Lesson Five

Every Crisis Creates
a "New Normal"

Life is what happens when you are busy making other plans.

—John Lennon

As we move through our lives, the big-ticket disasters—sickness, getting fired, loss of a partner or friend, having to move—come along with more frequency. "Death has become a ubiquitous presence, like a lazy yellow jacket," one woman said. "In the past three years I have lost my best girlfriend, my husband, my nephew, and now am watching my dear sweet mother take her last steps. The causes of death are compelling—heart attack at 48, car wreck, ovarian cancer. The grief," she adds, "is fear, pure and simple."

Over time, things do, as my friend Maddy says, "look darker." "Yes," we hear ourselves say with increasing frequency, "but consider the alternative." Loss and crisis are part of the picture, but so are coping, improvising—and recalibrating. Accepting what one must and accumulating the wherewithal to take on what has to change are necessary attributes of Second Adulthood.

"Forging on," as Maddy calls it, as opposed to "moving on," which doesn't sound proactive enough for her.

Dottie was literally pulled from her roots just when she was getting ready to tend to them. But she forged on.

When my husband lost his job soon after our nest emptied, I felt totally lost. I had been looking forward to some time to fix the house up and devote myself to my hobby, quilting. Instead there were two years of his sending out resumes all over the country—no one seemed to want to hire a fifty-plus financial officer. He finally got an offer in Boston, a city I had never even been to. But we sold our house and moved up there. We were slow making friends, and when after a year, he was downsized out of the new job, we felt really lost. Another year of resumes later, he got an offer, this time in Canada. I just couldn't bring myself to move again, so we agreed that he would take the job and commute on weekends. That left me fending for myself.

One day while in the fabric store, I met another woman who quilts. She invited me to join her "quilting bee." At a meeting soon after that, one of the women talked about her nephew who had visited an orphanage in Africa where the children had no toys. We got the idea of making dolls out of our quilting scraps and sending them to the orphanage. The children were so grateful and so needy that soon we were selling the quilts we made to raise money for them. The next thing we knew, we had to incorporate our group as a not-for-profit—something none of us knew anything about then, but we sure do now! And last summer the eight of us took a trip to Africa to visit "our" orphanage. Who would ever have imagined that all those random events would lead to such an adventure. And, yes—my husband still has the job in Canada.

June* was sideswiped by cancer just as she was planning to take her time making plans for the rest of her life. Instead she *found* the rest of her life. For her, the agent of self-discovery was, of all things, the cooking channel.

I retired from the Army after putting in my twenty years and was expecting to take it easy for a while. That was not to be. I was soon diagnosed with breast cancer, and went through months and months of worry and treatment. As I was recovering, I had to stay in bed for weeks. To distract myself from my worries I started watching the cooking channel. I'd never been into cooking, but I got really hooked on the shows. I thought, "Hey, maybe I should go to cooking school." As soon as I was well enough, I signed up. I loved it! But I didn't discover what I really loved until the very last course—ice sculpting! And I'm really good at it. I put an ad in the paper and I've gotten enough orders to put me in business. I can't believe what's happening!

Coping is a lost-and-found department of sorts. Losses like Dottie's and June's are not uncommon; finding ways of reorganizing our lives to deal with those losses is where the ingenuity comes in. Not just once, but over and over again. Writer Alix Kates Shulman lives with the challenge of establishing a "new normal" every day.

When Alix remarried twenty years ago, hers was the ultimate

midlife love story. At a high school reunion, she remet Scott
who had been a football hero back when she was a cheerleader.
He was now a financial executive, and she was a fifty-two-year-
old almost-divorced writer and mother. Scott courted her with
ardent determination. They were blissfully happy together, even
more so after Scott retired and became a serious sculptor. Then
one night while they were at their vacation home in Maine, he
got up to get a drink of water and fell from the loft where they
slept. He hit his head and suffered brain damage.

With time and physical therapy he recovered enough to
communicate his affection but remained in need of continual
nursing and encouragement. Alix devoted herself to that job
with the same degree of ardor that he had devoted to courting
her. In her book *To Love What Is* she describes the frustrations
and setbacks as well as the wonder of adapting and even finding
joy in their days together. Their "new normal" is the accretion
of those small triumphs and heartbreaking disappointments.
When Scott couldn't walk, that became "normal" for a while;
then he could walk, but he wandered off and needed constant
supervision—and that became normal. When Alix came to
the realization that she would never again be able to count on
Scott—sweet and loving as he is—as an equal partner, that
became normal too. She reconstructed her own life so that it
included work and friends and distractions. And she forged on,
cherishing the good days and coping with the bad. It was "much
better than the alternative."

Improvising is the name of the game. Luckily, we are
increasingly well prepared for it; for one thing, we are increasingly clear about where our energies should be focused—What
Matters—and what is not worth "sweating"; and we are increas-

ingly adept at mobilizing those efforts with authority. We can deal with loss because we are becoming familiar with the mixed blessing—melancholy, perhaps, but also liberating—of letting go. We let go of our children; we find ourselves. We let go of some body standards; we become more comfortable in our own skin. Some of us let go of driving ambition, while others let go of the tentativeness that held us back from setting our ambition loose. We let go of outdated pipe dreams and we let go of material things. Every to-do list we compile includes cleaning closets, and although we rarely get to them, the fantasy expresses a very real drive to get rid of old shit and make room for something new.

The "new" we are accumulating fortifies us for situations we had never imagined we would be able to navigate. Our emerging defiance, for example, says no to people who are hindering our way to an important outcome and gives us courage in situations that our gut tells us need to be challenged. In the process, we are becoming comfortable taking risks, and we are better able than ever to withstand skepticism from others. There is also a growing confidence that we can roll with the punches, that we can turn the glass from half empty to half full. The anthropologists, who are documenting the power of postmenopausal women in various cultures, call it "mastery."

If that sounds like Mother Courage, someone too strong, too brave, too optimistic, that's only because I'm describing a good day. We all know about the bad days: being totally thrown by an embarrassing mix-up or your back goes out or you push the wrong button and your computer crashes just when you are putting the final touches on a report. Even on the good days many of us hear a little voice that keeps up a litany of dire possibilities that may lie ahead. In the next five minutes even.

I know that voice of doom as the Under Toad. A creation of novelist John Irving in *The World According to Garp,* he was the result of a misunderstanding by a child named Walt. Walt's family spends a lot of time at the seashore, and his parents are constantly reminding him to watch out for the undertow. One day they see him staring intently out to sea:

> *"What are you looking for, dummy?" Duncan asked him.*
> *"I'm trying to see the Under Toad," Walt said.*
> *"The what?" said Garp.*
> *"The Under Toad," Walt said. "I'm trying to see it. How big is it?"*
> *And Garp and Helen and Duncan held their breath; they realized that all these years Walt had been dreading a giant toad, lurking offshore, waiting to suck him under and drag him out to sea. The terrible Under Toad . . .*

That slimy, unspecific, menacing Under Toad wakes me up at night, blows its chill breath across my heart when the phone rings, laughs sardonically when I catch myself admitting that I feel—dare I say it? No!—happy. "Poo . . . Poo . . . Poo," my mother-in-law used to say to fend off the evil eye.

In my personal letting-go agenda, getting some distance from him is a high priority. Free-floating anxiety is, I tutor myself, a waste of time. As Gestalt therapy founder Fritz Perls taught, it is a rehearsal for the future, which, as we all know, never comes in the form we have rehearsed for. I also remind myself that I will most likely be able to cope with what comes, which almost certainly won't be the thing I was dreading, the same way I have coped with what has already come. There is no future in anticipating the worst.

Fearing the worst implies an equally unrealistic expectation of the best. Letting go of that one takes guts. Carly Simon, interviewed on her sixty-first birthday, said, "I used to have anxiety, now I have depression." She is famous for her bouts of stage fright (aptly called performance anxiety), a fear of not measuring up to expectations; now that the anxiety is gone, and the expectations are gone too, she seems to be struggling to fill the place where the worst and the best were. Germaine Greer writes in *The Change* about taking that next step: "Once we lose our sense of grievance everything, including physical pain, becomes easier to bear. . . . As we hoist in the fact that happiness is not something we are entitled to, or even something we are programmed for, we begin to understand that there is no virtue in being miserable. We can then begin to strive for the heroism of real joy."

The only place with real possibilities, Perls emphasizes, is the present. I have begun fending off the Under Toad by waving a coffee mug I found with the inscription "Every day is a gift. That's why they call it the present."

My friend Maddy has reached that same conclusion by more than her share of firsthand experience with the new normal. There might always be "a cliff with a loose rim" where she is about to step, she acknowledges, but she keeps going anyway. Not because she is brave, she insists, but because she is considering the alternative. "I figure that whatever happens is the hand I've been dealt, and I'd better make the most of it." The hand she has been dealt so far includes her mother's suicide, her own mastectomy, a bitter divorce, the death of a brother, and currently her husband's battle with prostate cancer. She recalls a moment of clarity twenty years ago, as she was being wheeled into surgery for a biopsy on her breast: half groggy from anesthesia, she was mumbling fervently, "Please, God, don't let it be cancer." Then she remembers reconsidering her prayer because, as she, ever the pragmatist, puts it, "God already knew whether it was cancer." So instead she rephrased her request: "God," she appealed, "give me the strength to cope."

And cope she does. Then and thereafter. As her friend, I have been part of one of her most effective survival strategies: managing her own caretaking. When she had her mastectomy, for example, she assigned everyone in her inner circle a task: someone to organize a week of rotating dinner providers while she was bedridden; someone to handle well-meaning phone calls; someone—that was me—to take her to the hospital the night before the surgery; someone to pick her up from the hospital. It was a win-win experience. She got taken care of the way she wanted, and all of us had the satisfaction of being useful. We also got another gift: her uncanny casting sense reflected how well she knew and treasured each of us.

Psychiatrist Sarah S. Auchincloss, who counsels people with life-threatening disease, has found that one of the most difficult challenges for a woman who needs help is to ask for it. "An even bigger challenge is for the woman to 'accept' what she needs from someone who's giving it to her, whether they're giving it because she asked or because they figured it out on their own." She tells her patients, "You really do need to try to tolerate it when people give it back to you; your job is to accept it."

Robin, whose life was turned upside down by that wayward e-mail, had to overcome her reluctance to share her problems and to accept the support she was offered. When she did, a therapist and her friends—and *his* friends—got her through the aftermath of her breakup.

>*I really did think "I have my friends, and I have my own way of reasoning, and I have my own way of thinking and I don't need a therapist." But the weird thing that happened was, one day I was at a client's, and she's this really like tough-talking girl, she's very funny, and I got this phone call, from him, and I was very short with him; I hung up the phone and she said to me, "What's going on?" And then she looked at me. "You know, what? I'm not going to ask any more questions. I'm going to e-mail you three names," she said, "I've seen more shrinks than anyone in the world, and I'm telling you if you need someone to talk to, contact the first name on the list." I went to see her. And she was wonderful; it was amazing, and I now believe, I truly believe in the benefits of therapy. I know now that you can talk to people you are really close to, but it's not the same as somebody that you don't know.*

>*I had these little angels, who appeared just when I needed them. My friend Robert is one of those people. He's gay; he's from the Midwest, and I know this sounds like a generalization, but you know how those people from the Midwest are just so pragmatic? One day I'm freaking out and Robert looks at me, and he goes, "Okay, so you are going to torture yourself to torture him? That sounds like a plan." Then he says, "I want to tell you something, you either go there and move yourself out, or you know what's going to happen? She's going to pack your stuff up, and she's*

going to move it out." Then this other very close friend of mine, Carol, says, "Contact him, tell him you want access to the place, and get your stuff out of there." And she drove in with my brother-in-law, with like twelve of those big storage bins, and they filled them up and carried them out.

And after that one by one his friends reached out to me, and I had more invitations than I knew what to do with, and I have developed relationships with all of them, better relationships than I would have ever had if I'd been with him. And it's been great because you know it was hard. I was happy to have all that—it made me very social; you just feel so sad, you feel so dropped, I just couldn't believe how great it was to have like a lot of people to be with.

I used to feel that people take advantage of people with good natures. I guess in a way I felt a little like maybe ashamed of the fact that I would always do things for people. Even from a little kid on, I had my father and my older sister, and my mother would be like, "Don't let them boss you around." But people came through for me through this thing. . . . You know, you do things for people when they're your friends, and you know that they'd do it for you, or you think they'd do it for you, but you hope you're never going have to test that, but so many people came through for me that now I don't even care what anyone says to me about doing things for other people; it's like, "That's what we do." That's what life is all about.

There is an ironic obstacle to getting the help you need. Many women, Dr. Auchincloss has found, have trained "their nearest and dearest so successfully to expect to be taken care of, that when the woman herself gets sick, she's just surrounded by a lot of dumbfounded people who have not got a *clue* what to do to begin to be able to take care of her." Again and again, Dr. Auchincloss has heard of such women saved by the same resource Maddy mobilized so efficiently, caring friends: "The woman is brought home from chemo by her well-intentioned husband, neighbor, whoever to the house where no one has done anything to deal with dinner that night, and there isn't any food and she can't cook and she's trying to figure out what they are going to do when the doorbell rings and it's the woman friend who has figured out that she is going to be home by then, and they will need to eat and she has brought dinner."

In the end, Maddy insists, "I am still luckier than most people. I have a family, I have my grandchildren, I have education, I know people who can help me, I have an interesting life, I have my garden." Her contentment reflects a hard-won faith in her inner resources and the blessings of her life, faith in her ability to accept the hand she is dealt, faith in her ability to take care of herself, protect herself, enjoy herself. It used to be called "self-confidence." It is the attitude that trumps circumstance.

Bernadette has it too. She calls it *intentionality*. Until recently she worked as a dental hygienist for thirty years to support herself and her son after her husband decided that "married life wasn't all it was cracked up to be." When he left, she was devastated; she didn't even tell anyone what had happened. "How can Prince Charming walk out on Cinderella?" she wondered. Then she wised herself up. "I knew the bubble was bursting and that I'd really better grab the bull by the horns," she says. By the time her son went off to college fifteen years later she was forty-eight and ready to get on with her own life.

But "life happened." Barely a year later, her ninety-one-year-old father took a fall.

> He had become senile, and when he fell he broke himself in so many places that we wound up hospitalizing him and he never came out of the hospital. But the day he fell was the day they diagnosed my 91-year-old mother's cancer. So at that point I made a decision to turn the lock on the door of my apartment and move back home, so that I could take care of my mom, and help her get in and out of the hospital to see dad. Then, on the morning of their sixty-second wedding anniversary in June my father passed away, and that was the week before my mother was scheduled to start chemotherapy.
>
> At that point I had already left my job, and I decided just to leave my apartment, because my son would be home in the summer, and as a young adult he might not want to spend all of his time living in his grandparent's home. I just stayed with my mom. And we got her in and out of chemo, and we did all the things that we did, but of course she was not going to recover, she had cancer in her bladder and her kidney. My mother was certainly more comfortable having me there to take care of her than to have either of my brothers to help her on and off a commode.
>
> Then, the week before my mother's ninety-second birthday, in January of 2003, she started receiving all these cards, and they were obviously birthday cards. So I'd say to her, "Hey, mom, you got a card, you want to open it?" And she said, "No, I never do, I always save my cards for the morning of my birthday. And then I sit down and I read my cards

and I have my breakfast." I said, "Well that's what we'll do." So on the morning of her birthday I took the cards to her and we sat down on the bed and we opened them. She would look at the envelope and say, "Oh, that's from Aunt Marie, you know this one's going to be all flowery with ribbons and everything." And the next one, she'd say, "That's from Peggy, and that one's going to have little cartoon characters on it." She knew just by looking at the handwriting who the card was from and what it was going to be like; she was a scream. I read all of the cards, and she decided she wanted a piece of rye toast with a little bit of butter on it, and a cup of coffee for breakfast. I went down and made the coffee and buttered the toast, and brought it back up to her and she'd gone to sleep and died. So, talk about symmetrical—you know? She was married and widowed on the same day, and born and dead on the same day.

When it came time to deal with the family's house, one of Bernadette's brothers urged her to stay on, saying he was sure their mother would want her to move back to the old neighborhood. That sounded good to her, but accepting the offer meant getting a new job. One day she went to get a manicure at the local strip mall and she noticed a dentist's office upstairs. She went up and asked if he needed a hygienist. He couldn't believe it—his current employee had just told him she didn't want to work weekends anymore. So Bernadette had a job. "All my life," she says, "I've stepped out and there's what I need right in front of me; a life of intentionality I like to call it."

She worked evenings in the dentist's office and spent several afternoons a week baby-sitting for a niece's baby. She was settling into a pleasant life. Then two things happened: the niece whose baby Bernadette had been caring for became pregnant with triplets, and she offered to hire Bernadette to care for them; and her brother announced, to her dismay, that he needed the house back for his stepson. What appeared to be an amazing stroke of luck produced an offer of another house down the street at a bargain price, but the good fortune was not as random as a more self-pitying person might think.

An important component of Bernadette's intentionality is her own instinctive investment in "what goes around." The house belonged to a neighbor, Mary, who had been very kind to her father when he was in the late stages of Alzheimer's and other neighbors were shunning him because of his inappropriate behavior. After Mary's husband died, Bernadette returned the kindness. "On Fridays I'd pick Mary up and two of her cronies and they'd get their hair done, and we'd go to the supermarket shopping and we'd go out to lunch." Mary was getting ready to go into an assisted living facility at the same time as Bernadette was being evicted from her house. Mary offered hers to Bernadette. "I could manage if I could get this much money"—a lot less than the market value of the property. Even so, it took some big-time loans and the cooperation of a brother who cosigned her mortgage, but when Bernadette "stepped out" this time, it was into a new house and a new job description: nanny to triplets. "I do what I do on the weekends, and during the week I'm Aunt Bern and the nanny."

Interwoven throughout this saga are childhood friends who are still in the picture, neighbors, even her ex-husband, and a one-time boyfriend with whom she has a "love/hate relationship. I love him to death, but there are things about him that I can't stand. I won't say we talk every day, but we certainly talk every week." And there is Bernadette's attitude. "I truly believe that if people take on a 'woe is me' attitude, then 'woe is me' is what you're going to live. Over thirty years of dental hygiene, you get to meet a lot of people, and you get to see a lot of human nature, and it's all that story: if you were in the room with ten people and everybody put their troubles into a pile, you'd probably pick out your own again.

"You know," she adds, "you've got to look at the situation and cut your losses."

When things go wrong, "woe is me" is one pitfall. Blaming yourself is another. Dr. Auchincloss finds that it is important "to get past a woman's desire to self-destruct trying to repair things, and past her desire to turn everything about her into a criticism." That is particularly true for those confronted with two of the most common and most unwelcome losses of Second Adulthood: getting divorced, as in Robin's case, and losing your job.

Getting fired can be a particularly bitter challenge because the situation may be so unjust, the anguish so unnecessary, and the economic consequences so catastrophic. Because of the politics of the workplace, older workers are eased out, so are women who may have been the last hired and become the first fired, and those who seek the flexible hours of a more humane workweek are often considered troublemakers. This is how one Horizontal Role Model created a satisfying "new normal" from that particular blow:

Being unemployed for the first time in my life at age 53 hurt. Hurt even worse, as my resume and cover letter got me into interviews, even repeats, then having to come to realize no one seemed to want to hire someone as "experienced" as I. (One time after interviewing for a job, an ad popped up in a local paper for that exact job, only now they were looking for someone with 5–10 years of experience—not my 20+ years experience.) After a year, I was lucky to finally find another job, through an employment agency, by doing a temporary stint, then ultimately getting hired at a school at a low level position. I have the summers off without pay but am able to keep the insurance going for a modest monthly fee. So I decided to accept this new situation (albeit not by my choosing) as having my life "reinvented" to enjoy the summers off for the freedom this offers; started watercolor painting and doing some quilting, along with taking short trips to the Maine coast.

For many a divorcing woman, job anxiety strikes when she is most vulnerable. Rebuilding a life often requires finding a job or a better paying one very quickly or having to move to a new town or all of the above. A note from another Horizontal Role Model makes it sound easy, but it took years until she finally saw the gleam of a light at the end of the tunnel; when she did, though, it turned out *not* to be, as a woman in similar circumstances worried it might, "another train coming toward me."

I lost my job in NYC and went through a divorce three years ago, so I sold my condo and moved to Philadelphia without knowing a soul—just packed up my cat and my stuff and left. I was out of work for over a year, and it was really rough for a while, but I didn't regret my decision to

go; I needed the emotional break from dealing with an
emotional batterer (my ex-husband) and the bitterness of
losing a job at a company where I worked for 14 years.

  Now my grown daughter is living in NYC with her
husband (and they're expecting my first grandchild which is
FANTASTIC!). But no one is financially dependent on me
anymore—well, nobody but the cat.

  Now I am dating a man 14 years my junior who makes
me laugh every single day, and I'm actually considering
marrying him, something I thought I'd never do again. . . .

When disease strikes, the new normal of being a patient
bears no resemblance to the old normal. Neither does the
patient's relationship to herself. Jungian analyst Jean Shinoda
Bolen calls cancer "the wisdom disease" because its serious-
ness combined with relatively slow progress forces the victims to
assess their lives.

Poet Audre Lorde's breast cancer ultimately got the best of
her (she died in 1992), but before that, she found wisdom in her
struggle to recalibrate her relationship to life, death, and fear.
Early on in her treatment, she wrote in *The Cancer Journals:* "I
am not feeling very hopeful these days, about selfhood or anything else. I handle the outward motions of each day while pain
fills me like a puspocket and every touch threatens to breech the
taut membrane that keeps it from flowing through and poison-
ing my whole existence. Sometimes despair sweeps across my
consciousness like lunar winds across a barren moonscape."

Eighteen months later she achieved a new perspective.
"Sometimes fear stalks me like another malignancy, sapping
energy and power and attention from my work. A cold becomes

sinister; a cough, lung cancer; a bruise, leukemia. Those fears are most powerful when they are not given voice, and close upon their heels comes the fury that I cannot shake them. I am learning to live beyond fear by living through it, and in the process learning to turn fury at my own limitations into some more creative energy. I realize that if I wait until I am no longer afraid to act, write, speak, be, I'll be sending messages on a Ouija board, cryptic complaints from the other side. When I dare to be powerful, to use my strength in the service of my vision, then it becomes less important whether or not I am unafraid."

Lorde's consciousness shifted from what is wrong with me? to what is still right? In a crisis, emotional survival depends on establishing a new normal every day. "It's not a total transformation," Dr. Auchincloss observes, "but the metabolizing of what somebody's been through, the damage assessment, the figuring out what is most important, that includes a lot of letting go—of perfections that are no longer attainable, and mistakes made along the way. People get better at just not obsessing about that stuff because they really see, 'I've got something special here,' you know, 'I'm around, I'm not in treatment. I'll just be using my energy better.'"

The wisdom that comes from attentive engagement with adversity is hard-won and precious. The four Horizontal Role Models who wrote *This Is Not the Life I Ordered* consider it so important to preserve an awareness of what you are capable of that they recommend maintaining real-time contact with yourself as you go along. When things are bad and you are losing it, they suggest writing letters to people who are important in your life. "Tell them what you are going through, how you are feeling, what you have done to attempt to cope. Then seal the letters. Don't send them yet. After you have successfully managed this transition, reread the letters. Write the ending to the story and share your lessons learned. At that point, decide if you wish to share your journey with the special people you wrote to."

Dr. Auchincloss points out a crucial coping mechanism that deserves to be celebrated: "I'm actually beginning to wonder if it is possible that human beings are hardwired to make jokes in bad situations. Is there any way that the primate specialists could enlighten us on this? We can all see that what it does is change the situation so you're seeing it from a direction you can handle. I think black humor is just a godsend; it's really an *invaluable* resource in most adversities."

It seems to me that our karma these days is to explore in more depth than ever before the two sides of letting go. On the one side is the shedding of excess emotional garbage: the abandonment of lost causes, the downgrading of expectations, and the acceptance of the losses that time brings. On the other side is the letting go that enables us to move beyond those losses. Reduced expectations, for example, free up the imagination for new experiments. Getting through the bad times enables us to take our measure and focus on what really matters going forward.

THE LESSON: Every encounter with adversity leaves you far from the place you were on the way to. But coping with the unexpected also brings self-discovery and empowerment. And a keen awareness of What Matters. Each "new normal" offers new opportunities for a first step toward the next. Those include opportunities to ask for—*and* accept—help. By putting one foot in front of the other that way, you will generate the momentum to keep going.

Do Unto Yourself as You Have Been Doing Unto Others

*In the unlikely event that oxygen is required, secure your own
mask over your nose and mouth before helping others.*

—Airline emergency instructions

S elf-discovery can feel like selfishness, which is, for many
of us, something to be ashamed of, so we back off. What's
more, the upheaval that accompanies new behavior can
frighten those who love, work with, and count on us, and they
may react in unexpected ways that undermine our efforts. In
addition, the "sandwich generation" experience—the increasing
needs of parents we thought we had outgrown and the resurg-
ing needs of children we thought had outgrown us—can challenge a woman's efforts on her own behalf. Yet countless women
aboard the bumpy flight that is reinvention are finding that by
putting on their own oxygen masks first, they are able to map a
personal trajectory across the longitude of their own well-being
and the latitude of important others in their lives.

Ava* who has just turned fifty, had plenty to contend with

even before the bitter meltdown of her marriage left her financially strapped and emotionally wiped out six years ago. She
has three children, one of whom is autistic. For ten years she set
aside her career as an attorney to care for him and build awareness of—and, finally, literally build a school for—autistic children, which her son attended until he was eighteen and moved
to a boarding facility. Yet when everything fell apart, she kept
going, and as she dealt with the crises in her life, she also made
choices that, as she now sees it, were personally supportive. "I
did take care of myself," she says, "in terms of looking for the
things that made me feel good about myself."

> When I went back to work the main reason was finan-
> cial, but I also had to decide whether I wanted my life to
> revolve around autism or to build something for myself. It
> was hard to get back into the work force. It did seem over-
> whelming. But I really didn't have a choice. Ultimately it
> was the best thing I ever did; it was one of the things that
> kept me sane and functioning.
>
> It enabled me to focus on myself and build my own per-
> sonal confidence—I was contributing to society, but also
> developing my intellectual abilities, my ability to support
> myself. I had done a lot in my autism world but it didn't tap
> into the intellectual side or financial side.
>
> As for relationships with men, I dove right in. It was
> another confidence thing, to feel that there were other peo-
> ple who were interested in me. Given the challenge of jug-
> gling all this stuff on my own, I was careful to pick people
> who were not demanding but were there for support, com-
> panionship and to have fun with.

Running was the other thing that made me feel good about myself. I had been a runner—I did the marathon in 1986—but not always at such a high level. After the divorce, I started to run more—about five days a week. I run partly because it physically makes me feel good, but also because running was the only time I could be by myself. I generally run alone and listen to music. I go and run for an hour and no one bothers me. When you are running you are able to block out the world. I think, listen to music and just sort of put myself in another place. I have a knack for long distance running, so I can just keep going. It invigorates me. It gives me a sense of serenity—maybe it's the endorphins, but whatever it is, it is one of my real saviors.

I am finally at a place in my life where I do feel things are adding up. I was pretty overwhelmed for a long time, though I guess I was functioning at a pretty high level. I feel good about where I am now. I am better off being out of the marriage I was in. I am very pleased with how my children are doing. I am very pleased with my profession. I feel good physically. And I'm enjoying the ability at this stage of my life to begin new relationships and to start fresh on the terms I want. I didn't' realize that until very recently— maybe it's the person I am with—a good part of getting divorced is that you have the opportunity to get to know yourself better—you're not just part of a team, you're more your own person. And being stronger as a person makes for a much better relationship, more mature, no baggage. It's wonderful

So yes, I guess I have taken care of myself.

Many women need a wake-up call before they get to the point where Ava started and begin to factor themselves into their own lives, consciously, or, as Ava insists in her case, unconsciously. My favorite story about altruistic excess is Michealene's lice disaster. She tells her story in *This Is Not the Life I Ordered;* it begins with "the dreaded pink note my three young boys brought home from school. It's the note that makes any mother shudder: head lice had struck the classroom." Her sons had not escaped. For a week she was washing all the sheets daily, treating her kids, checking her husband and even the dog. When the scourge had passed, she was exhausted and looking forward to the camping weekend the family had planned. But rest was not to be. "During our second day in the woods, I began to feel ill. I also found tender lumps behind my ears and in my armpits," she recalls. When she began to run a fever, she decided it was time to get to the emergency room. Waiting there, she thought of "twenty-five terrible diseases I just knew I had. I thought of my children and my husband. How would they manage without me?"

When the ER doctor called her aside for his diagnosis, she was petrified. "My suspicions are confirmed," he began ominously. "You have one of the worst cases of head lice I've seen in twenty-five years." Her symptoms were an allergic reaction to the bites. A lightbulb lit up. "I had checked everyone in the household—even the dogs—but I had never once checked myself." Michealene had learned a crucial Life Lesson. "My mistake was creating a to-do list that didn't include me!"

If we really mean to do unto ourselves as we have been doing unto others, we have to counteract this kind of self-neglect. One remedy is a regimen of well-placed "not nows" and "not anymores." "Not now"s recalibrate interpersonal timing. An interruption asserts one person's need for something—even if it is just an answer—over that of the person who is doing something else. Babies interrupt all our activities, including our sleep, with their needs, but in many families such demands become entrenched. And the fulfiller is usually the same one person. I can't forget Mary Catherine Bateson's description, in *Composing a Life*, of the moment she suddenly realizes that throughout their twenty-year marriage, whenever her husband interrupted her, she put down the book—or thought or task—she was engaged in and snapped to attention; whereas when he was engrossed in something, she was totally accepting of his "Not now." Reclaiming our time, our concentration, our privacy is a first step toward doing unto ourselves.

Reclaiming our own priorities is harder. That's where "not anymore" comes in. It goes without saying that there will always be responsibilities we willingly assume for the caretaking of others and there will always be generous and helpful things we *want* to do for those we cherish, but that still leaves many errands, favors, and managerial functions that could be shed. They get in the way of burgeoning maintenance duties, delightful indulgences, and general organizing that we need to attend to for ourselves in order to take advantage of this important transition in our lives. How many times, day after day, have I postponed something as simple as washing my hair because family requirements came up that pushed it (me) off my to-do list? I have a friend, an inveterate list maker, who is trying to break this habit by beginning her daily back-of-an-envelope assignment sheet with one to-do for herself. Even if she already has several agenda items for others swimming in her head, she will not relieve the pressure by writing them down until that first one is in place. She intends to keep this up until she learns to check in with herself every day without prompting.

My guess is that it won't be any time soon. Old habits hang on. Just the other day I almost sacrificed a book I was enjoying reading on the subway (on a day of multiple subway rides, I might add), because my husband said he *might* be home early and *might* have some time to start reading it himself. I *didn't* leave the book for him, and what's more I realized that he had never asked me to; that was all my idea. Not anymore.

Another way we can do unto ourselves is by putting ourselves out there. Stepping up to the plate. Calling attention to our accomplishments and capabilities. We are masters at imbuing someone else with what it takes to stand out; we earned those credentials on the job or in the relationship where we were head cheerleader and coach, bucking up flagging confidence and stoking the fires of risk taking. The classic example is the woman who has volunteered for political campaigns all her life—knocking on doors, arguing forcefully for her candidate's positions, working through the night on campaign literature, keeping the team going despite bad news or unfavorable odds. But when her candidate moves on or gives up, does she ever put herself forward? She can't imagine asking for money—for herself—or arguing policy—about her own ideas—or urging the staff on—to help *her* win; it's "not her style." It is almost inconceivable for most of us to go after power on our own behalf.

But with a little prodding and a lot of what anthropologist Margaret Mead called "postmenopausal zest," women are becoming more self-assertive; some are even becoming the candidates they would have worked for. A critical mass of women—though nowhere near 50 percent—is forming in high-level state and national positions, and those mayors, governors, congresswomen, senators are becoming Horizontal Role Models and mentors to local charity fund-raisers, school board delegates, and community troublemakers. It's an uphill battle, according to Kathleen Sebelius, governor of Kansas. When you ask for people to step up to a challenge, she told *More* magazine, "The guys who are dumb as a desk will have their hands in the air, saying, 'Take me, I'm ready.' Women think, 'When I take the next three accounting courses, then I'll be ready.'"

Several organizations, including Emily's List and the White House Project, were designed specifically to train women in the basics of articulating forceful positions on the issues and asking for money and votes. They soon discovered that they also have to flush these women out of the woodwork. One organization, the Women's Campaign Forum (WCF), launched a recruiting drive based on the idea that every woman has at some point said of another woman, "She should be running this town." Anyone can nominate that woman—or herself—on the organization's Web site. Then the WCF contacts the nominees, checks them out, and encourages the best prospects to stand for an appropriate office.

When you combine the breakthroughs that Second Adulthood women are making for themselves—speaking truth to power, embracing new challenges, and developing a Fuck-You Fifties stance of independence and authority—with the worldly experience, confidence and know-how they have accumulated so far, you have a potent recipe for a hot candidate. Or CEO. Or movie producer. Or construction mogul.

Or neighborhood angel. An unpaved street got Lois going. "Our street hadn't been paved since the eighties, even though they made many promises," she says. She decided to tackle the problem the way she did in her office job: "The buck stops with me. So one day I said, 'I've had it.' I went and got thirty-five signatures from my neighbors. I was like their angel. I brought a sample of the road to the mayor—I brought gravel and rocks, because this was my evidence. I said 'Here's a petition I have that we want the street paved.' He said, 'You didn't have to go through all that.' I said, 'Number one, I like the exercise. Number two, I met neighbors I didn't know. And number three there's more power with numbers.' Now my street is going to be paved. If I had just sat back and complained like everybody else, nothing would have been done."

Efforts to get ourselves back on our own radar screens get a boost from—once again—the hormonal adjustments taking place. It is as though nature is on our side, gently prodding us off the sidelines (at the metaphorical nurse's station) and onto the playing field. With menopause "the ovaries have stopped producing the hormones that have boosted her communications circuits, emotion circuits, the drive to tend and care, and the urge to avoid conflict at all costs," explains Dr. Brizendine. "The circuits are still there, but the fuel for running the highly responsive Maserati engine for tracking the emotions of others has begun to run dry, and this scarcity causes a major shift in how a woman perceives her reality. . . . She's not getting the calming oxytocin reward of tending and caring for her little children, so she's less inclined to be as attentive to others' personal needs."

For many of us, it is just at that point—when we are downshifting our caretaking engine and revving up our personal priorities—where along come aging parents with an increasing number of personal needs and an increasing irritation at us, their children, who are trying (a tad resentfully) to fulfill them. Sociologist and psychologist Lillian Rubin has been writing about family dynamics for four decades. Now eighty-three, she has just sold her first painting and written her twelfth book, *Uncharted Territory: Living the New Longevity,* the premise of which is "Getting old sucks!" Part of what sucks, she argues, are the demands of intergenerational caretaking, common situations in which some people her age are caring for their spouses—her own husband has Alzheimer's—and/or being cared for by their children. She is particularly insightful about the common and painful crisis of assessing a parent's competency. Children "think they see the line [between competence and losing it, between living on their own and assisted living] more clearly" and "push their parents to a decision, mostly out of loving concern but also because they need some relief from the worry and the burden," she writes. But the parents push back. They "resist as long as they can, not generally because they don't trust their children and their motives, although that's undoubtedly true in some cases, but because with each step of their decline, they fight ever more tenaciously to hold on to what's left. Their sense of self, their self-respect, demands it." Is it being selfish to make the pragmatic decision here?

Caregiving can impinge on our ability to do unto ourselves financially as well as emotionally. A recent survey reported that the average annual outlay for the thirty-four million Americans who care for an elderly relative or spouse is $5,500, twice previous estimates and more than the same family spends on health care and entertainment combined, and up to $8,728 when groceries, out-of-pocket medical costs, and transportation are factored in. Where do those dollars come from? Loans, skipped vacations, ignoring their own health-care and retirement savings. And the time—from twenty-three hours a week among higher-income families to forty-one among those who can't afford to buy services—where does that come from? Income-producing work, personal care like exercising or eating healthily, private time, and other relationships.

Needless to say, the vast majority of those donating their time are women (indeed a primary determinant of whether a parent will spend his or her final years at home rather than in an institution is having daughters and daughters-in-law). If you know one, help her break out of the guilty or desperate assumption that she can do it all herself and that she is being "selfish" for just thinking about relief. If *you* are one of them, find a group (there are many online resources) or person to whom you can admit your "bad" thoughts and burned-out circumstances; ask for help and then *let* your community help you put your oxygen mask on.

Caretaking way beyond the point our hormones prepared us for and at the expense of our recently retrieved independence creates a fiendish bind. How, we despair, can we do unto ourselves under these grinding circumstances? We ask ourselves another question too, one that has the potential for answering the first—how can we avoid repeating those circumstances when our time comes? "I don't want to end up like that," we say of pitiful decline. "I don't want to be a burden on my children." What exactly do we mean? I used to think that we were testing the notion of taking one's exit into one's own hands. That may be part of it, but in terms of what we can prepare for now, it also means wanting to be able to call the shots more effectively when our time comes than our parents have.

Looked at this way, a major component of doing unto ourselves has to be tending unto our own future needs with as much attention as the caretakers among us are doing unto others' current needs. The details of daily maintenance and the bureaucratic sinkholes will eventually pertain to us too. Here's the tough love version of what's at stake: the emotional renewal that comes from harnessing your inner resources for your own nourishment is well and good, but unless you address the equally urgent need to take charge of your in-the-world life, you are wasting your time. This urgency applies even more to women who are still building equity and earning power than to those of us who have less time and fewer resources to work with. Yet it is hard to get their attention. Ava, who was so good at taking care of her emotional and professional life, didn't want to hear about planning for the future. "Retirement and the realities ahead seem far off to me," she said, "and not something I am thinking about or particularly want to read about."

The efforts required are personal, but also communal and ultimately also political. At a recent lecture about considering retirement, the speaker urged the rapt audience to consider whether they had more than a vague notion of the practical realities ahead. The room was silent for a long time. As always, the answer lies in more questions:

- **Where Will You Want to Live?** And how do you want to live—alone or with others (friends, family, like-minded contemporaries)? And how does that situation compare with your current one?

- **How Long Do You Plan to Work?** Do you know whether you have the choice? Do you want to change the kind of work you do? If so, will you need training? Or if you want to start a business, how long will it take to get on your feet?

- **How Much Money Will You Need to Manage?** Do you know how to go about figuring it out? If not, do you know where to go for help? And what sources will that "paycheck" come from? If you don't have an adequate nest egg now, what can you do between now and whenever?

- **Have You Got Your Safety Nets in Place?** What kind of care (insurance, trusted advisers, medical team, support group) have you provided for yourself?

- **Have You Made Your Wishes Known?** What kind of care or support do you want to provide for dependents? What provisions have you made to ensure that your medical directives are on record?

- **How Would Your Answers Change** if your circumstances changed from being a partner to being alone— or vice versa?

It may be hard to project your lifestyle into the future, and it will take some industry and discomfort to achieve the expertise you need to get real about it. The simple question of where you will live, for example, generates myriad hard truths. For one thing, it is reasonable to assume that sooner or later each of us will have to design a new living situation for herself. The statistical likelihood is that whether or not we are living alone now, half of us will be widowed or divorced by age fifty, and most of us will get there eventually.

If we are forced to think about that eventuality, *The Golden Girls* model—a compatible group of buddies who keep one another company, support one another's endeavors, share chores, and laugh a lot—is a favorite fantasy. But the reality of such an arrangement is much more complicated. If they want to make it work, the roommates will, among many other contractual obligations, have to draw up a prenuptial-like life-sharing agreement that anticipates what they will do if one gets chronically sick or loses her income or another wants to sell her share.

Usually, though, making do as needs arise is the typical—and unreliable—pattern. Seventy-two-year-old Pat has made it work—so far. "I've learned to accept help from friends," she says. "We—a group of about eighteen, mostly women, but a few men—kind of help one another out. It used to be that I would tough it through. Like if I got up in the morning and the car wouldn't start, I'd walk to work. I don't do that anymore. I'll call somebody. Or if they have a problem, they call me. We have a support system among us. And we're kind of learning as we're going along."

What is an exercise in improvisation for Pat is, for Charlotte Frank, a challenge in need of a game plan. The vibrant colors she typically wears reflect her bright outlook. She is a born organizer who approaches life's transitions with an eye for building and sharing resources. She has been doing that throughout her Second Adulthood. After retiring from her executive job, she cofounded The Transition Network (TTN), "the first resource exchange and support community for women with skills, energy, and expertise who wanted to keep using those skills in new contexts." Over the subsequent ten years she devoted her own skills, energy, and expertise to growing TTN into a nationwide organization. During the same decade she has moved on in her own life and is looking at a new kind of transition: from independence to support.

Recently Charlotte, who lives alone and has no children, had a short-term illness during which she needed some help from her friends and neighbors. That experience inspired her to find out how it was for other women in her situation. Some clear and recurring themes emerged: "They found asking for help too personal and an imposition on others," she reports. "And they admitted that offering help is not necessarily easy either." To capitalize on the evident willingness to help and answer the occasional need for help, what was needed was a blueprint for mobilizing a community's resources in times of crisis. Charlotte set out to draw one up: a pilot program to engage The Transition Network in helping members who have health problems and also to turn her New York City apartment building into a "vertical caring community."

As a compact among the program participants, she has chosen the model of time banking and barter—"hours given in service to others will be banked for hours of care in return"—that has worked in several other communities. To help her neighbors make the most of available resources, she is developing guidelines for using organizations, such as the Visiting Nurse Service, and ferreting out lesser-known organizations that can play a part. One she found provides emergency-response training for building employees, who are often the first ones called. And she is becoming expert on the programs that are being devised to support the so-called aging-in-place movement.

Her goal, she says, is to "demonstrate that informal communities are an essential part of the health-delivery system. What better place to start than with the organizations one belongs to and the place one lives?" Specifically the pilot program will "test ways to engage management, develop a data base of emergency contacts, determine and handle liability issues and organize residents so they see themselves as real neighbors" as well as "a service corps." The practical objective is to have a plan in place that will gear up as soon as it is needed. It anticipates typical problems, like taking someone to a doctor's appointment or to the supermarket, or help coping with a sinkful of dishes or a plumbing disaster. Everyone who signs up to participate will know what they are expected to do, and every tenant will know what they can expect from the community.

What a given woman thinks about "retirement" is a determinative issue, even before the financial calculus comes into play. It affects the decisions we make about where we will live and exposes a whole new array of emotional needs. Working plays such a big part in most women's lives that the option of giving it up engages a panoply of life-long patterns and personal affirmations as well as hopes and fears. As Jeri Sedlar and Rick Miners point out in their book *Don't Retire, REWIRE!* it is important to "know what you are leaving behind when you retire, then figure out how to replace that in the future." For many people the most important aspect of working, aside from money, is community. If work contributes mightily to our identity, we have to find ways for retirement to do the same.

For many that means retiring from one job but moving on to another. The one piece of good news for us in the job market is that due to a developing national brain drain, there are more and more openings for people who either have the skills (usually "people skills"—our specialty—for service jobs) or are willing to retrain. Flextime is becoming a more realistic option. Largely because of the difficulty of replacing enough of their income, the percentage of people over fifty-five in the workforce has gone from 18 percent in 1986 to 29 percent in 2006. Many of them are reinventing their work life. I recently read about a couple who both left high-pressure sales positions and retrained as a driving team for eighteen-wheelers.

No matter what models and dreams we are able to articulate and even map out, the sober truth is that all Yellow Brick Roads need a stop sign at the bank. And the financial picture for older women is not good. Nearly one-third of single women over sixty-five are classified as poor, and it isn't entirely their fault. "The reality of women's lives makes it almost impossible for them to save adequately for retirement," says Laurie Young, executive director of the Older Women's League (OWL). "It's not because they're doing anything wrong." She adds, "The system is really stacked against them." To cite just two statistics: although we are likely to live seven to nine years longer than the men in our lives, we are unlikely to have a pension plan. For every year we have left the workforce to care for a child or a parent, it will take five years to make up the difference in our retirement and pension plans.

To make matters worse, nearly every woman who has reached her Second Adulthood has brought along some kind of major hang-up about money. The two most common are the core conviction that she just can't understand the math (because she is a girl) and the bag lady syndrome, a recurring nightmare that no matter how hard she works, she will wake up one day sitting on the curb with nothing but the few possessions in shopping bags beside her. These hang-ups and most of the others I have heard have one assumption in common: that a woman's financial fate is out of her control, in the hands of some version of a white knight or fate itself. One woman, who was doing pretty well until she had to max out her credit card with charges from unexpected dental surgery in 1999, came up with a unique fantasy. "When the millennium happened," she says, "I was praying that it would wipe out all the credit card information." Turning around this paradigm of helplessness is one of the most troublesome requirements of inventing the rest of our lives.

Lois, for example, who had the self-confidence to mobilize her neighborhood to get the road paved, goes limp at the prospect of getting her bigger, and potentially profitable, dream off the ground. "What I really wish I could do is open up my own day-care center for animals. But it takes a lot of money. You have to have insurance. I would need backing. It's hard to find it. Everybody has a dream. That's why I play the lottery."

After writing seven books on the subject, personal finance guru Suze Orman thought she knew everything about money and how people dealt with it. So she was shocked to find out that women she actually knew, many of whom were very successful executives who managed big budgets for their companies, were, like Lois, secretly freaked out at the prospect of managing their own finances. And that they were freaked out in a gender-specific way. In her eighth book—just for women—Orman becomes a passionate voice for doing unto yourself. "I find the core problem to be universal: When it comes to making decisions with money, you refuse to own your power, to act in *your* best interest. It is not a question of intelligence; you absolutely have what it takes to understand what you should be doing." So what is it? "You simply won't bring yourself to take care of yourself financially, especially if those actions compete with taking care of those you love." You can surely see the Life Lesson coming. You must, Orman urges, get over doing "for everyone before you do for yourself."

My friend Angela* really hit bottom a couple of years ago. Her "absolute biggest financial blunder was self-delusion and false pride. I pretended that I knew more than I did, because I didn't want to appear 'stupid.'" What did her in was, she admits, "letting my heart rule my head."

> *I was involved with a man who made a great deal of money and who was very generous to me. I assumed I would always have him as my "safety net" if things really went south. We had, in fact, invested in several things together that had done very well. What I never planned or imagined was that he would end up bankrupt and in jail for financial misconduct—and that his fall from grace would literally wipe me out as well.*
>
> *Not only did I lose the money we jointly invested, but during his fall, I tried to help him by lending him a large sum, because I truly believed that he would be able to regroup and recoup his losses. Neither happened.*
>
> *How many times while growing up had I heard wise women say, "Don't mix love and money"? I had always followed that rule until I fell head over heels in love. And, boy, I've been beating myself up ever since.*

Looking back, she joins the chorus of women who wish they had taken the trouble to get good financial advice.

Although I had saved what I thought was a good chunk of money, I never really factored really rainy days into my financial planning: Never planned on spending a huge sum providing round-the-clock care to maintain my mother in her home during her last year of life. Never thought that I might lose my job—I did. Never thought that I would hit a wall when I had to look for a new job—I did. All of those events—the tech stocks, the man thing, my mother, my job loss—were happening almost simultaneously, and I was reeling emotionally. I realize now that even then had I the presence of mind to seek financial advice I might have been able to stave off disaster. But I didn't.

An AARP survey found that most women weren't sure whether their finances would carry them through any one of Angela's tribulations, let alone the rest of their lives. Some felt that no matter how well they had planned, they might "outlive their money." Baby boomers, in particular, were uncertain about their ability to get out of the credit card hole they knew they were in; other respondents fell back on the weak hope that "things will work out" for them. Obviously, each of us—and I am speaking as loudly as I can to myself *and* to Ava—needs to sit down with a book or an adviser or an accountant or a savvy friend and go over the numbers, the insurance policies, the retirement benefits, the health plans, the credit cards.

This isn't an easy conversation to have with an expert, and even harder to have with a family member. Jackie, another coauthor of *This Is Not the Life I Ordered,* remembers vividly her attempts to discuss his life insurance with her husband. "I kept nagging him to renew it. He told me he was too busy to take the required physical exam. He got tired of me bringing it up and yelled 'Jackie! Are you planning to have me done away with? Is that why you are so persistent about this?' I dropped the subject. Three months later he was dead; I was left with an unborn child and a five-year-old. I had less than forty-five days to vacate our dream house on Chateau Drive—a house I could no longer afford." She went through a grim couple of years and now uses her story to galvanize other women for whom it is not too late. "Today I play back that conversation about life insurance in my mind . . . I wish I had said, 'Steve this situation is not about me. It is about our children and their quality of life if something happens to you. I am not being morbid. I am being financially responsible.'"

Responsible is the operative word here. Doing unto yourself is not "about me"; it is about taking practical and emotional responsibility for the rest of your life. Yes, it includes mastering your checkbook and managing your health, but it also includes healing the past, revising life patterns, and responding in the best way you can to what every day brings. Not long ago I heard the Dalai Lama describe the tenets of Buddhism. One insight struck me as especially apt. "You are your own refuge. You are your own master." If we neglect either of those capabilities, we have little to give ourselves—or anyone else. Women who are experiencing both—nurturing themselves on their own resources and reveling in their own mastery—find that the process actually takes them out of themselves. The more enriched and empowered they feel, the more effective they can be in the world and the more engaged in making things better for others. Generosity, not selfishness, is the impulse of a well-tended self.

THE LESSON: Taking care of yourself has nothing to do with selfishness and everything to do with survival. It is not about self-indulgence but about taking responsibility for your practical and emotional life. To make your garden flourish, you need to nourish your roots, prune wisely to strengthen your stalk, and pick your fruits with care. You also need to be ready to protect yourself, not just everyone else, when the weather turns bad.

Age Is Not a Disease

"My best friend tells me that when she apologized to a Scottish friend for forgetting something, saying she had had a 'senior moment,' her friend said, 'They're not called that anymore. They're called CRAFT.'

" 'What's CRAFT?' asked my chum.

"Scottish lady replies, 'Can't Remember A Fucking Thing.' "

"OK, I've got one you won't believe," I announce to my once-a-month dinner partners. They all lean forward. "Dry eyes!" I crow. In our ongoing update of the "challenges" our bodies have come up with (partly, I suspect, to make sure the latest infirmity is "normal"), I have delivered a doozie. While checking the drugstore shelves for contact lens lubricant, I saw a whole array of products labeled "for dry eyes due to aging." Who knew? While we were watching our waists disappear and our necks pile up in folds, our eyes were drying out! Every day in every way our bodies confirm the wisdom of the anonymous woman who said, "Don't take yourself too seriously; no one else does!"

The ironies abound. Just as we are getting more emotionally and psychologically daring, some of us need to be more careful physically, holding on to stair rails, not running for every bus, switching from the treadmill to the elliptical trainer. Just as we are becoming more comfortable with who we are inside, disconcerting external signs of aging can make our appearance unrecognizable and undermine our self-confidence.

On the other hand, our brains, our sexual lives, our sense of our place in the world, despite dwindling capability and drive, reflect an invigorating rise in a sense of mastery. We are simply better at living than ever before.

The trick, according Dr. Sherwin Nuland, is to "play only to our strengths." His advice applies beyond the limits of the physical body. "Some of the more meaningful of those strengths may be not at all less than they once were. The later decades of a life become the time for our capabilities to find an unscattered focus, and in this way increase the force of their concentrated worth."

The "postmenopausal zest" Mead identified—the delicious enjoyment of new horizons, uninhibited self-expression, and general enthusiasm—is part of our energy profile too. We are heating up in more ways than one. (There is a wonderful T-shirt emblazoned with the slogan: "This is not a hot flash! It's an energy surge!"). The message that *you are not who you were, only older* applies in two very important ways when it comes to your body. For one thing, your body is not simply falling apart—*only older;* it is regrouping and your relationship with it is becoming more focused and mutually supportive. Many women even find that as a result of an awakening respect for their bodies and their well-being, they are in better shape than they have ever been. At the same time, you become aware of new dimensions to your physical being. The sensual pleasures and athletic challenges that matter to you now are different from the ones that were paramount when you were *who you were* at earlier times in your life.

I keep meeting women who have discovered the joys of salsa dancing or the vacation possibilities of serious hiking or biking. Others, like Ava, keep on running with more focus than in the past. I also know women for whom physical changes have a ripple effect on their lifestyles. For Tichrahn, who sees her Second Adulthood as a spiritual journey, "Adapting to the changes gravity brings and altering our exercise routines is important to stay in tune with our inner voices." Her new routines are gravity-friendly and spiritually energizing. "I enjoy my walks in the woods, always discovering new energies in new secret places, helping me stay connected to the land and the inner voices of creativity. I also ride my bike in the park. The wind in my hair and freedom of riding lets the child within flow and reaffirms the guidance of play."

Mary is having a little more trouble finding her own "gravity-friendly" reality to replace an outgrown athletic fantasy. "I have this idea in my mind that before puberty I was athletic and an outdoorsy type. I have had the adult-life yearning to get that feeling back again, but there seems to be quite a bit of interference from my left brain. It says, 'Stay inside or watch TV or spend time on the computer.' Someone told me one time that I need to plant my bare feet on the ground and pay attention to how that feels more often. I am honestly working at it, now that

I have semiretired, but boy, there is a foggy spot in the brain that really avoids physicality whenever it can."

Aging is not a disease, so caring for our bodies is not about restoring or curing breakdowns but about enhancing and maintaining those strengths that Dr. Nuland talks about. It is also about developing better communications skills with our corporeal selves, picking up the messages that will help focus our attention where it's needed.

We know something about maintenance from the effort we have been putting into the lesser ruffles and flourishes of our appearance all along. We are all too familiar with the escalation of cosmetic maintenance, from simply getting our hair cut to restyling it, conditioning it, and eventually coloring it. Or skin care. From washing to cleansing, to moisturizing, to deep moisturizing, to peeling, and on and on from there. Over the years, such maintenance becomes more intense, more time-consuming, and—around my group's dinner table—often more absurd. (An African American friend of mine points out that in at least one respect, she is exempt. When I commented on her wrinkle-free skin, she replied, "Everybody knows that black don't crack.")

The other and increasingly crucial kind of maintenance is even more time-consuming and expensive. It includes the regular checkup, the "just to check things out" follow-ups to that: a mammogram, a colonoscopy, and a complete exam by a dermatologist. (Recently such an examination revealed a melanoma on the *bottom* of a friend's foot.)

The notion of active—or mindful—maintenance came home to me at the end of just such a visit. The dermatologist was in the process of exploring my scalp like a loving lemur when I drummed up the courage to ask him about trying Rogaine, the hair-restoring treatment, for my thinning hairline. I was really hoping he would confirm what well-meaning friends had been telling me—"I don't know what you are talking about!"—rather than what I saw, albeit in the magnifying mirror. Or if he confirmed my observation, I hoped that he would say that he knew of some medical-grade version that would restore my hair to its former glory. His response was none of the above. "Sure," he said. "Try it. Even if you don't get much regrowth, it will keep it from getting worse."

"But," I whimpered, "I hear that you have to keep doing it for the rest of your life." "Right," he said. "It's called maintenance."

With that conversation my understanding of what was required of me by my body shifted. Although I had been trying to shed responsibilities, this is one I would have to take on. A healthy lifestyle is not enough. Staying well requires vigilance and aggressive attention to preventing things from deteriorating more or faster. Mindful maintenance. As Dr. Andrew Weil puts it, the notion of "aging gracefully" is not about expending great amounts of precious energy—our "zest"—fighting the process, but in letting "nature take its course while doing everything in our power to delay the onset of age-related disease."

If there is a mantra that applies to just about every challenge of Second Adulthood, from dealing with our loved ones and reinventing our lives to managing our health, it is the familiar Serenity Prayer: Give me Serenity to accept the things I cannot change, Courage to change the things I can, and Wisdom to know the difference. Discerning the difference between age-related inevitabilities and conditions that need attention is a skill we need to polish assiduously and continually. For example, while my thinning hairline is par for the course, if I develop bald patches, they may be a sign of an autoimmune disorder. Likewise, while a pot belly is hard to avoid, weight-gain farther down may increase the risk of heart disease and diabetes. Expect yellowing teeth, but red gums are a sign of gum disease. And so it goes.

"Though age may not necessarily bring wisdom, age nevertheless demands it," writes the good Dr. Nuland. "At earlier stages of our lives, things tend to take care of themselves. They do not require the consistent attention and watchful circumspection we come to need in order to negotiate our later decades."

A common mix-up between the must-accept and the must-deal-with can lead a woman whose libido seems to be disappearing to conclude that her sex life is over. But thyroid problems, depression, diabetes, medications (including, ironically, antidepressants) are just as likely to be the—treatable—cause. A particularly down-to-earth example of the importance of discerning the difference was cited by a woman doctor I talked to: "You talk about those things we can change or just have to accept," she began, "but I do want you to know that a leaky bladder is not one of them. In fact I left my eighteen-year career as a regular gynecologist to become a subspecialist in a new area of GYN called urogynecology that treats that area especially." She is one of many women doctors who are finding personal and professional satisfaction in taking care of women like herself. "I love working with—and hanging out with—women my own age," she explains with a smile.

The Serenity Prayer omits one crucial piece of wisdom: the life-enhancing benefits of *laughter among friends*. A parody of the Serenity Prayer makes up for this failing. Called the Senility Prayer, it goes like this: "God, grant me the senility to forget the people I never liked anyway, the good fortune to run into the ones I do, and the eyesight to tell the difference."

While each of us is making the necessary adjustments to what is happening to her body, the body itself is in a dynamic maintenance mode. It is making adjustments of its own to overcome some of the limitations that age brings. The brain, for example, develops myriad fail-safe systems to back up any slowdowns in the front office. Women are especially well endowed in this department; throughout our lives, our brains show much more communication between the hemispheres than men's, and many more areas of the brain are involved in standard functions; an age-related failure or weakening in one area will be compensated for by the well-established ancillary systems. Since I often find myself hesitating to begin making a very interesting point in a conversation, because I can't see a key word ahead in my mind, my favorite study of the compensation phenomenon is about vocabulary. I found that while we do indeed *lose* words while we are speaking, we also *use* many more words overall than we did when we were younger. In other words, the brain backs up the one lost word with a whole thesaurus of synonyms that become available as we talk.

In an essay called "Song to Sensuality," Maya Angelou identifies another reconfiguration of physical input, a new dimension of pleasure that is very personal and profound. "I have reached the lovely age where I can admit that sensuality satisfies me as much as sexuality and sometimes more so," she writes. "Leers and lascivious smirks to the contrary, sensuality does not necessarily lead to sex, nor is it meant to be a substitute for sex. Sensuality is its own reward. . . . I like the tomato-red dresses of summer and the sienna of a highly waxed mahogany table.

I love the dark green of rain forests and the sunshine yellow of a bowl of lemons. Let my eager sight rest on the thick black of a starless night and the crisp white of fresh linen. . . ."

The message here is that physiologically we are in a reliable holding pattern of wellness that, if mindfully maintained, will sustain us until we really become sick. To cite just one example: while heart disease becomes the number one threat to women as we age, the heart is not running down. "[T]he most remarkable characteristics of the cardiovascular system's response to aging are the two . . . it shares with all other organs and tissues of the body," writes Dr. Nuland. "Its extreme variability from one person to another and its continuing competence to do its job perfectly well under normal conditions, even when it can no longer deal as effectively with major challenges."

But how do you know whether the "continuing competence" is being threatened? Learning to read the messages that the heart, to stay with that example, is sending requires that all-important skill of "knowing the difference," partly because we are only beginning to understand how the female body "speaks" (most studies of disease were male-only in the past). And because we have spent so long speaking harshly to our less-than-perfect-looking self, we are not used to listening. The symptoms of heart attack in women are extremely subtle, easily pooh-poohed by a busy woman and dismissed by her doctor. Many women let warning signs, like vague malaise or back pain, go on too long for fear of looking silly or bothering the busy doctor.

Offering herself as a Horizontal Role Model, one woman was so anxious to get the message out that she blanketed her e-mail universe with the story of how her body communicated "heart attack." In her case, the symptoms were not as subtle as they often are, but they were still not the chest-clutching kind we see in movies. Her account also has some pointers for that all-alone-when-it-happens situation we all dread.

I was sitting all snugly and warm on a cold evening, with my purring cat in my lap, reading an interesting story my friend had sent me, and actually thinking, "A-A-h, this is the life, all cozy and warm in my soft, cushy La-Z-Boy with my feet propped up." A moment later, I felt that awful sensation of indigestion, when you've been in a hurry and grabbed a bite of sandwich and washed it down with a dash of water, and that hurried bit seems to feel like you've swallowed a golf ball going down the esophagus in slow motion, and it is most uncomfortable. You realize you shouldn't have gulped it down so fast and needed to chew it more thoroughly and this time drink a glass of water to hasten its progress down to the stomach. That was my initial sensation—the only trouble was that I hadn't taken a bite of anything since about 5:00 p.m. After that had seemed to subside, the next sensation was like little squeezing motions that seemed to be racing up my SPINE (hind-sight . . . it was probably my aorta spasming), gaining speed as they continued racing up and under my sternum. This fascinating process continued on into my throat and branched out into both jaws. AHA!! NOW I stopped puzzling about what was happening—we all have read about pain in the jaws being one of the signals of an MI [myocardal infarction] happening, haven't we?

I said aloud to myself and the cat, "Dear God, I think I'm having a heart attack!" I lowered the foot rest, dumping the cat from my lap, started to take a step and fell on the floor instead. I thought to myself, "If this is a heart attack, I shouldn't be walking into the next room where the phone is or anywhere else . . . but, on the other hand, if I don't, nobody will know that I need help, and if I wait any longer I may not be able to get up in a moment." I pulled myself up with the arms of the chair, walked slowly into the next room and dialed the Paramedics. I told the operator I thought I was having a heart attack due to the pressure building under the sternum and radiating into my jaws. I didn't feel hysterical or afraid, just stating the facts. She said she was sending the Paramedics over immediately, asked if the front door was near to me, and if so, to unbolt the door and then lie down on the floor where they could see me when they came in. I then laid down on the floor as instructed and lost consciousness. I don't remember the medics coming in, their examination, lifting me onto a gurney or getting me into their ambulance, or hearing the call they made to the ER on the way. But I did briefly awaken when we arrived and saw that the cardiologist was already there in his surgical blues and cap, helping the medics pull my stretcher out of the ambulance . . . I nodded off again, not waking up until the cardiologist and partner had already threaded the teeny angiogram balloon up my femoral artery into the aorta and into my heart where they installed 2 side by side stents to hold open my right coronary artery.

Staying with the heart for the moment, Joanne* experienced an attack of a totally different kind. Her body was trying to tell her something vital, but it took her a while to make the connection between her body and her soul.

> *Over the last year, I've ventured back into the dating world (!). When the relationship was emotionally healthy, I physically was fine. However, in two different relationships my body became ill when the relationship was ill.*
>
> *During the first relationship, I developed mono (!) and also awoke with a collapsed radian nerve that resulted in weeks of therapy. As the relationship dissolved, I physically felt stronger.*
>
> *My second relationship lasted for about six months. The irony is: the week of its demise (which was a quick demise, not one of mourning while still being involved), was the very week I was back at the doctor's having learned I had an internal infection.*
>
> *So my lesson is to listen to my body as I consider getting involved again—my body appears to know what I choose not to recognize.*

Another woman has made an art of connecting her physical symptoms to her state of mind. "When I get a urinary tract infection, for example," she explains, "I know I am pissed off about something, and I have to figure out what."

The I-told-you-so role that Joanne's body played in her wake-up to bad choices has wider applications and implications than most of us recognize. We can't remind ourselves too often that stress—the body's cry for help from life's pressures—throws off our equilibrium. Stress also makes it harder to pay attention to what our bodies are telling us; it disrupts and discourages our mindful maintenance and ultimately makes us sick. Getting sick can be a last-resort effort to escape stress. "The major advantage of illness is that it provides relief from responsibility," writes Dr. Gordon Livingston. "Of all the burdens that weigh on our lives, being responsible for ourselves and those we care for can be the most onerous. People endure numbing routines, jobs they hate, unsatisfying relationships, all in order to fulfill the expectations they have of themselves. When no other relief is available to us, some form of illness or disability is one of the few socially acceptable ways of relinquishing the weight of responsibility, if only for a little while."

One of the benefits of Second Adulthood is a stress-defusing outlook: a desire and a growing ability to not take lesser things too seriously. "Let it go," we say. And we take a deep breath. Breathing is a perfect metaphor for the equilibrium that mindful maintenance is all about. It is a unique physiological activity, in that the movement of every breath captures the balance between mind and body, between letting go and taking in; it is the function that most reflects the body's ability to take instruction from the conscious mind and at the same time to regulate itself. Deep breathing is also one of the best antidotes to much of what ails us.

A seldom-surveyed contributing factor to a sense of well-being may be, despite conventional wisdom, good sex. I have heard a lot about sex in this strange new world of Second Adulthood. The responses can be sorted into three general categories: "Who needs it!" "Where do I get it?" and "What took so long?" (Perhaps this is the next-stage version of the question we posed in a memorable cover line on *Ms.* magazine back in the seventies: "How's Your Sex Life? Better / Worse / I forget.")

The first two categories are self-explanatory; the third—"What took so long?"—is the one we need to talk about. There are countless Horizontal Role Models out there who have told me how, to their amazement, sex has become not only better, but very different for them around menopause. For some the simple knowledge that pregnancy is no longer an option—or a risk—is so liberating that they feel more relaxed and better able to focus on their pleasure. Others say that their Fuck-You Fifties have taken on a literal form of expression. Many women are ready to throw themselves into sexual experimentation and self-expression. And still others have told me about their discovery of "casual sex" or "sex for its own sake"—the kind of sex we disparaged in men.

A physician whose practice consists primarily of postmenopausal women makes a point, which other doctors rarely do, of questioning her patients about their sexual satisfaction. She finds that when she puts the topic on the table in a safe and relaxed environment, women have lots of questions about how to make the most of their bodies' changing sexual responses. For those who are feeling inhibited, she admits, "I often recommend pot." She also discusses vaginal lubricants and masturbation as well as testosterone (to boost desire) and estrogen replacement therapy (ERT), about which we all seem to be still very confused. I know women who went off hormones because of news reports only to find themselves desperate to go back to them and others who are happy to be "clean." Several women gynecologists have told me they have prescribed ERT for themselves because for them quality of life issues outweigh the statistical risks. And I know physicians who shake their heads mournfully at the very mention of estrogen. Now there is the whole new bioidentical hormone community vying for our attention. It seems to be every woman for herself on this one.

A widely praised 2006 movie called *Heading South* purported to explore this counterintuitive sexual exuberance. It features three mature white women who frequent a Haitian resort where women like them engage beautiful young black beach boys, giving them money, gifts, and doting admiration in exchange for hot sex. The amazing Charlotte Rampling stars as a Wellesley professor who has enjoyed playing the boy-toy game for several years until a rival arrives at the resort, and jealousy drives her into wanting a relationship with her favorite. At this point, the emphasis of the movie shifts from the fresh theme of celebrating lust among midlife women to the more traditional cliché of rivalry between women. The joyous, liberating, self-empowering sexual experience the women characters talk about is made to seem pitiful. The message is that no matter how hard women try to talk themselves out of competing for men or into enjoying simple delicious sex, no matter how liberated they think they are, the need to possess the beloved or to beat off a rival will win out in the end.

I have gotten just the opposite message from women who have sex with men, or women, with whom there is nowhere to go but back to bed. Jealousy and possessiveness are tired old themes, to be dealt with if need be, but the real headline is the s-e-x. For them, being old enough to know what they want and being able to go out and get it is so new and so titillating that it opens up an endless array of delicious possibilities. As I keep discovering, women are finding that getting to know your new/ older body is not only about aches and pains.

There is one message, though, that enough of us aren't getting. The magazines we count on for guidance aren't broadcasting it, and we are not picking up on it in our conversations with one another: *Women over fifty are at an increasing risk of HIV. The heterosexual transmission rate has doubled in the last ten years, and women like us are not getting tested.*

Nancy Cosentino, an elegant woman in her early sixties, became an expert in this subject through the most unimaginable sequence of circumstances. Several years ago her daughter, Regan Hofmann, discovered that she was HIV positive, the result of an ill-fated relationship with a totally respectable man she would, she says, "date without hesitation today." It was agonizing for Regan to tell her parents that she would be HIV positive for the rest of her life, but she finally did. For Nancy it was hard to accept the news and, like her daughter, it was also very hard to share it with her family and friends. They were sympathetic about the fact that her child was very sick, but they had no point of reference for the disease. It was a taboo subject that had no place in their world.

In the intervening years, Nancy has learned a lot about HIV and about the ignorance among women like herself. What started as a catastrophe has given both mother and daughter a shared mission and bond of mutual respect and devotion. Regan is now the editor of *POZ,* the magazine for HIV-positive men and women, and Nancy is devoting her time to alerting other "respectable" women to the real danger of not protecting themselves against the virus.

In our generation, safe sex meant birth control, which was first the diaphragm (remember that?) and then the Pill; condoms were what boys kept in their wallets for back-seat-of-the-car opportunities. By the time AIDS came along, many of us were in settled relationships with habitual forms of birth control and had no occasion to use a condom. As we move into menopause, we assume that since we can't get pregnant, we don't need to "use something." Those of us who are divorced or widowed have enough problems getting back into the social swim to even think about the ickiness of learning to use a condom, let alone asking a man if he is HIV positive. According to an article in *POZ,* "Even women as young as 35 to 54 were much less likely to ask about their partner's sexual and drug use history than women 20 to 34."

This is very risky behavior. Menopause causes dryness in the vaginal walls, which can be damaged during intercourse, making it more possible for the virus to enter the woman's body. A new sex life with new partners creates multiple opportunities for infection. Viagra has enlarged the pool of candidates with a past—from the midlife stud to the retirement community Lothario so common that he is known as a Condo Romeo.

Like many of us, Nancy had never discussed sex, let alone safe sex or HIV infection, with her doctor—only 38 percent of women over fifty in a recent study had done so. Women our age are likely to see doctors younger than we are, who may be as embarrassed discussing sex with someone who could be their mother as we are raising the subject with them. Even if they believe that anyone over fifty actually *has* sex, many doctors are as ill informed as their patients about what is going on. (They don't know, for example, that 65 percent of people in retirement communities report having regular sex, despite the unbalanced male-female ratio.) We are going to have to get the conversation going among ourselves.

No one has yet quantified the health-giving properties of the medical information exchange among trusted friends and Horizontal Role Models. When someone I know has a question or a problem, I find that the circle of advisers mobilizes quickly and often widens to include friends of friends who have been in the same boat—women at a full six degrees of separation who are prepared to share with a total stranger their expertise about the choices of treatment, the quality of hospitals, and such patient-tested techniques as how to manage a postmastectomy drain. We summon the executive skills to get one another through the torments of dealing with insurance companies. We accompany each other to crucial medical appointments and take notes, we monitor hospital care, we organize groups of friends into visiting nurse services, and we don't flinch at the sight of a bald head or mastectomy incision.

"Patients will ultimately be the stewards of their own health information," Dr. John D. Halamka of Harvard Medical School told the *New York Times*. "In the future, health care will be a much more collaborative process between patients and doctors," he added. Right now the opposite is true. The typical doctor visit is more like a slam-bam, thank-you-ma'am sexual encounter than a deep, meaningful relationship. Worse, some of the diseases most likely to hit postmenopausal women—diabetes, heart disease, multiple sclerosis—require visiting multiple specialists, who rarely compare notes with one another. That means it is up to the patient to keep track of what medications she is taking and make sure each doctor considers possible complications from any new ones. (I have yet to find a doctor who doesn't sneer when I list the supplements I'm taking, but Web sites are being developed that will enable us to check out interactions between both kinds of medication on our own.) She may find herself carrying X-rays from one part of town to another just to make sure that they won't have to be repeated. And there is always the worry that with all those specialists looking at their particular body part, a crucial symptom or condition, in an unclaimed organ, may be overlooked.

Marge worries about those of us "brought up not to question the doctor/god—a bunch of nonsense that needs to be erased from our collective consciousness immediately!" She learned about the dangers of blind faith several years ago when her sixty-three-year-old mother-in-law suffered a heart attack. "After she was released from the hospital, I'd call to see how she was doing. No matter what time of day I called, Pop said she was sleeping," Marge recalls. "On the third day, I asked, 'Pop, is Mom getting out of bed at all?' 'Oh, yes,' he said. 'She gets up in the morning, has some tea and toast, takes her pills and goes back to bed. I wake her at lunchtime, she says she's not hungry, but she gets up and sips a little soup, takes her pills, then goes back to bed. Same thing at supper.'" It turned out that due to an error in the prescription, she had been taking a sleeping pill four times a day instead of just once. "We each have to be the patient advocate for our own body," insists Marge. "We not only need to know our body, we need to know and understand the medications we take."

We could all use a doctor like Eileen Hoffman, whom I nominate as Horizontal Role Model for the profession itself. In her book *Our Health, Our Lives,* Hoffman describes her practice as an amalgam of "medicine, gynecology, and psychology with nutrition, exercise prescription, counseling and education." Her woman-centered orientation "takes into account 'sex,' which refers to women's unique biology, and 'gender,' which refers to women's unique experience as females in society." That whole-person approach should be the goal of every "collaboration" between patient and doctor.

"It is all right to be ill as long as you do not feel sick" is the conclusion of Harvard's Dr. George Vaillant, who analyzed every major longitudinal study looking for "indicators" for *Aging Well* (the title of his book). It surprised him to find that "objective good physical health was less important to success-ful aging than subjective good health." The 93-year old author of *Shut up and Live!* is a little less poetic in her rendition of the same message. "When two old people get together, they always have that *organ recital*. It's 'How is your bladder? My stomach is giving me fits. . . .' I want to change this scenario. Let's say, instead: 'How many miles did you do today? Is your bicycle in good shape?. . . .' As Maya Angelou says, 'I may have pains, but I don't have to be one myself!' " It seems ironic that having spent most of our lives pushing and pulling and putting down our bodies, we find ourselves doing all we can to support and appreciate the battered remains of that ungrateful abuse. On the other hand, the belated respect that we are beginning to show our stalwart physical selves corresponds to a reconsidered and generally upgraded evaluation of the rest of our inner resources. For perhaps the first time in our lives the two aspects of exis-tence are coming into harmony.

THE LESSON: The message that *you are not who you were, only older* has particular resonance when it comes to your body. It is necessary to acknowledge and tend to the changes that aging inevitably brings, but it is equally necessary to respect and support the positive adaptations your body is making to those changes. It is also increasingly important to learn to pick up danger signals from body *and* soul. Mindful maintenance is about the tiresome routines that are required to keep all systems at go; it is also about working with, around, and occasionally against the medical establishment, and asking questions about whatever is happening to your body until you have the answers you need.

Your Marriage *Can* Make It

A good marriage at age 50 predicted positive aging at 80. But surprisingly, low cholesterol levels at age 50 did not.

—Dr. George E. Vaillant, *Aging Well: Surprising Guideposts to a Happier Life from the Landmark Harvard Study of Adult Development*

O f all the renegotiated relationships taking place in our lives, the unavoidable recalibration of a long-term marriage is the most fraught and fragile. Unlike the adjustments between parents and children who are moving into their own lives, or the friendships that do or don't respond to changing needs, a long-term partnership is right there, on the front line of our efforts to redefine ourselves. Every role that has been written for women is in play, including the all-encompassing nurturer-in-chief. The relationship with a husband embodies our sexuality, our understanding of femininity, our domestic power, and if the marriage has been going on for a long time, the definitions seem carved in stone. How we deal with conflict, with exploration, with aging, with intimacy are ingredients in the simmering stew of a long-term marriage under review.

Of course, any change taking place in this most intimate of relationships is only a supersize version of our efforts to redefine intimacy with others very close to us: parents, children, friends, and siblings. Many of the growing pains—the need to get to know each other anew, the need for trusting respect for independence and personal space, the desire for a sense of authenticity on both sides—apply across the board. Those who are establishing new partnerships at this stage often find themselves grateful, as Ava does, to be negotiating these elements after having worked them out on their own first.

If a long-term marriage is involved, the emotional pot is simmering on a front burner. As they look to their marriage for, perhaps, the first time in years, the partners' circumstances are changing. In some cases, he is dreaming about winding down just when she is getting a second wind professionally. Or he is looking for domestic coziness just when she wants to see the world. Many women are not prepared to deal with the fact that rather than spending less time with a husband, the likelihood is more time together. In truth, many of us have lost track of what we knew about each other in the first place. Where, in the turmoil of inventing the rest of our lives, does he fit in?

As a woman I met at a sixtieth birthday party for a mutual friend, explained it, "One day I am full of ideas about how I want to spend the rest of my life, and the next day I am just as full of doubts. One thing I know: I'll be making some big changes—I can feel it." Then she paused: "But I don't know what this will do to my marriage."

Every marriage is mysterious in its own way. We all know of couples that seemed enviably supportive and loving only to blow up in bitter recriminations. By the same token we know odd couples—the smart, attractive, successful woman who stays with the philandering ne'er-do-well or the charming, gregarious, upbeat husband who stays with his sour, antisocial wife. We assume that one is putting up with the other, but given that it is all a mystery, it is just as likely that the reverse is true. Or there may be something that is very precious at the heart of their relationship—secrets shared, good sex, trust (even in the midst of betrayal)—that makes all the rest secondary. When Hillary Clinton wrote in her autobiography about the dynamic of her relationship with Bill that they had "started a conversation" in 1971 and it was still going on, she demystified that particular long-term marriage to my satisfaction.

Most of us in long-term marriages have, at one time or another, wondered what we were doing there. And as we move into this stage, we wonder if the changes we are making in ourselves will rock the boat right out of the water. "My husband married a very different woman from the one I am now," we say. What we really mean is, "If I'm becoming a different woman, what am I doing married to the same man?" Does a new lease on life mean having to walk away from a marriage of twenty or thirty years? Sometimes it does. Some women choose to leave—to escape constant conflict, deficient affection, emotional or physical abuse, simple emptiness. But for others of us, making changes in our own lives can energize and transform marriages that we can no longer live within, but don't want to live without.

For many women, the first challenge is getting the conversation started. We aren't sure how much we want our husbands to know about how pragmatically we are reviewing the marriage and how seriously we want to make changes. We also wonder about tone. As any coffee break conversation confirms, we talk differently about our husbands than we talk with them. And sometimes we just can't get their attention. "I wanted to talk about my increased restlessness with my husband," one woman lamented wryly, "but he was asleep on the couch." Even when partners are wide awake, some women may resent the prospect of once again doing all the "relating" in the relationship—just at a moment when they are eager, as one woman put it, "to go out of the emotional management business" and concentrate on themselves.

The couples who have gotten past those roadblocks to create a refreshed emotional contract of their own tell a new kind of love story—about making demands and practicing patience, about self-discovery within the familiar, about old truths and new agendas, about finding joy in the road taken. Here are five very different versions of that love story.

Lucy,* a social worker, has been married for twenty-eight years to a middle-school principal; they live in the Midwest and have two children now in their twenties. Some years ago, Lucy moderated discussion groups in a court-mandated program for divorcing couples. She saw "good people," she says, who become unhappy in their marriages and didn't speak up until their "hearts had hardened and they had moved away from each other." The experience prompted her to insist that she and her husband take a new marriage vow: "When there are pockets of time that you become unhappy, you will tell me." They often referred to this commitment, and it helped them resolve conflicts.

Until about two years ago. With midlife changes accelerating, Lucy began gently dropping comments like, "Gee, we need to start doing more things together" and "Gee, the kids are leaving home and. . . ." She didn't get much reaction. "So I changed my strategy. I told myself, 'He's an administrator, a bright man. I'm an educated woman who runs things. Let's approach it like a business.'"

First, she presented a basic assessment: "We have two girls we are getting ready to launch. We have lots of years ahead of us. We're still committed and want to stay together. But we are in a rut." Her husband agreed that he wasn't feeling good about things either, that he felt "drained." So Lucy challenged the two of them to take the step any smart business team would take: "write a mission statement" for the second half of their marriage.

"The starting point was to say, 'We still have a lot in common. We've worked hard, we've put the kids first—now it's our time,'" Lucy explains. Their goal, they decided, was "to celebrate and increase the enjoyment of and with each other." As they got more specific, it turned out that the list of things to celebrate included those they *didn't* do together. He was looking for more time to play golf with his buddies; she wanted time with her girlfriends. Lucy was struck by research showing that healthy people not only eat well and exercise but also have good social support. She realized that their busy schedules had kept them from doing much with friends. "So on our new list were the names of some couples we wanted to get to know better," she says.

And there was another element in the mix Lucy wanted to adjust: work. While her husband was looking forward to retiring and doing much of the cooking (and even housework), she was becoming more keenly involved in her job. Earlier in the marriage she worried that he felt threatened by her career; but at this new stage a revised balance felt comfortable. "I'm going to have to carry the ball—and the health insurance," Lucy told her husband. "That's fine, because I'm such a people person." But she wanted to change their rules for times when her job takes her to faraway conferences. "I didn't want to do it alone anymore," she told him.

When Lucy and I talked, she and her husband had just come back from a conference in England and she was exultant. He had come along for such events before, but on those occasions, she recalled, "I would feel like I needed to attend to him. This time I'd walk out of a session, and there he was meeting people. And when I was getting ready to do my presentation, I looked up and he was standing in the door with roses!"

Lauren* had less goodwill to build on than Lucy, despite a happy and egalitarian start to her marriage. She and her husband, both lawyers, had shared one job so they could do things together. But when their two children came along, and she cut back on work, they reverted to more traditional roles, and the marriage began filling with resentments. "Things moved from good to worse," Lauren recalls. Instead of relating to her and to the children, her husband "went into provider mode," becoming a workaholic and fitness addict.

Lauren hung in; she thought the kids needed two parents,

even if her husband was so seldom present that he amounted to "a quarter of a person." And there were moments when they reclaimed the old energy. "Whenever we went on vacation, we really enjoyed each other. On a certain level I really love him, and he really loves me. Even though I suffered from his not appreciating who I really am, I got a lot of 'Oh, you're so beautiful, you're so kind, you're just an amazing woman.'" And the sex was good. "Really great!" even during the bad times.

Turning fifty was a watershed for Lauren. She had always been "very assertive professionally, and successful," she says. But she discovered that she was tired of pushing, and wanted to use some of that boldness to new purpose. "I'm going to open up more space for myself," she resolved. She also wanted her husband "in my life more." As Lauren considered the changes she wanted to make in her "third act," her first impulse was the familiar "we need to talk" gambit. At dinner on vacation, she tried bringing it up. But her husband felt threatened, she says, "thinking that what I really was saying was 'I regret being married to a person like you.'" At one point, he panicked and suggested renewing their original marriage vows. "Are you kidding?" Lauren thought to herself. "Not until we work out, like, ninety-three new vows."

To get some distance, Lauren signed up for a trip to Peru with a group of women. It was the first time she'd been away for two weeks without her family. She climbed to Machu Picchu and participated in a spiritual retreat in the jungle. "By accident," she says, as if to explain why a rational lawyer would do such a hippie-dippy thing, "I signed up for some kind of crystal treatment. They shoot lights through you down your chakras; you're lying in this room, blindfolded, hearing this spooky

Peruvian music. I had no idea what was supposed to happen, but after about a half hour, I heard this voice that said, 'Do not die before becoming the person you were meant to be.'"

Wherever those words came from, it was the message Lauren needed to hear. "I became more comfortable saying, 'I'm not going to play inside that old pattern anymore.'" Her own calm surprised her and gave her the courage "to watch my husband freak out" as he saw her and himself in a new light.

Instead of focusing on changing her husband or her marriage, Lauren started acting on the new impulses she felt bubbling up inside. Many of them were about saying no. She spoke up at moments where she used to smolder silently, calling her husband on behavior she hadn't challenged before. To her surprise, she found that when she spoke up, she didn't get as angry, and the tone of her marriage began to change. He was "totally shocked. He hadn't seen himself as such a forceful person, and he thought I had been speaking up all along," she says. She realized that what she took for anger was often fear. "Honey, I'm not leaving you," she would tell him. "I'm just trying to tell you what I want."

Despite the soothing words, Lauren is on her own journey, she says, and she isn't about to turn back. "I'm trying to be nurturing, while at the same time saying, 'Uh-uh. This is how I feel.' It's a weird dance." And the sex is still great.

Maryl, whom we met earlier when she discovered her passion for photography, and Bill got married in 1961 at the end of the run for traditional marriages. "Bill was a Ph.D student and I had a full-time job to support us," she says. "And I had to do all the shopping, cooking, cleaning, laundry, ironing—in those days there was no polyester; I was ironing sheets, if you can imagine, at twelve o'clock at night!" Soon the turmoil of the sixties hit; "All the assumptions that people made about their lives were getting challenged," she recalls. "And a lot of people were getting divorced." Women she knew "would just explode because they couldn't stand whatever it was anymore, and they would just say they wanted a divorce." Maryl couldn't stand it anymore, but she didn't want a divorce either.

What she did want was "a high level of honesty and trust and discussion about our marriage"—on a regular basis. So she came up with the idea of an every-five-years "assessment of our marriage." Just before their fifth anniversary they took time out to prepare for the review by thinking about their gripes and concerns—"whether the marriage was working or not working, and if it was not working, exactly the way it should be so that it would work for each of us." Then they "came together, had the discussion," and by the time of their actual anniversary they had "rebonded."

She and Bill have repeated the process religiously for the last forty-five years. The issues that came up were "related to our social life and to sex, and to health and financial issues—the same things that probably come up for everybody," Maryl says. They have kept on track, even when they had to deal with the chronic sickness of their son and the demands of their work— particularly Bill's in the Peace Corps—which on occasion forced them to live apart. In retrospect, those separations actually reinforced the marriage. "We each had our very individual lives and yet felt our marriage was totally intact," she says. "And we loved being together when we were."

Not that they save up their problems for five years; they talk all the time. But the tradition forced each of them to look at the big picture and the long term. "We are really good com-municators," Maryl insists. "I would never think of keeping things inside. But it's much easier if you have this agreement in advance, and it's not related to any crisis. It removes a lot of negative emotion, because it is something that we agreed upon and we know why we're doing it, and we're doing it because we really love each other and we want to stay together, but,"—and this is the zinger—"we're not sure that we can."

Divorce has been "on the table" at every meeting, and on a couple of occasions, Maryl thought that it might be the best option for her. But they worked things out, and at their last five-year assessment, she realized that it was no longer on the table. Old grievances fell away and new plans flowed in. They had moved past the past and were focusing on what their lives would be like when they were not actively working the way they had been. "This is the first time we actually changed the format," Maryl recalls. "Instead of assessing everything, and saying what we would like to have changed, it was really what would we like the next five years to be. It was very positive, very wonderful, and very satisfying for both of us."

Susan and her husband, Alex, discovered that they had too much togetherness and not enough communication. They have no children, but they had their work. Soon after they were mar-ried, in 1985, they began writing together and produced two intensely researched and well-regarded books about media dynasties. Early in the marriage, to use a phrase they once used to describe another couple, they were "not just wedded, but welded together," says Susan. But after fifteen years, the stresses in their marriage reached a tipping point, and they began to move toward divorce. As Susan wrote, "We had gone through so much therapy and marriage counseling that we were practically *shrink*-wrapped. But we didn't seem to be getting anywhere. Working together had made us competitors and enemy combatants. Yet we never exploded, never shouted, never lashed out. Instead, we maintained a surface calm and suffered in silence."

Susan stayed in their New York apartment, and Alex moved to Boston; each began establishing a new life. But even as they made efforts to start over, both of them became aware of the love and history that was still there, under all the claustrophobia. They have now been back together for almost two years, and look on their separation as a kind of marital sabbatical.

The time apart unlatched the box they had trapped themselves in, full of labels and assumptions each had accumulated about the other. "You know, like 'You are always rude to my parents' or 'You never listen to my point of view.' Those recitations of 'always' and 'never' deny all the living and growing we've each done over twenty years," says Susan. Especially since there were no children to make demands and divert their attention from each other, when they reunited they had to take special care to establish breathing room in the marriage. As Susan sees it now, "We can cook dinner together, but we can't work together."

The fresh air also gave them fresh perspectives on the two people involved. "I realized that I wasn't the only one whose needs weren't being met," Susan concludes. "That in a marriage there is another person, someone who has a will and hopes and dreams that are exactly as valuable as yours. It is part of your job to make his happen and part of his to make yours happen. We understand the importance of being honest about what we are thinking or feeling. In some marriages, there is one Big Foot.

But not in ours. We were both just too polite to each other. A pox on that!"

Eve* has no problems with being too polite or not speaking up. Never did. Over the twenty-two years she has been married to Simon,* she has always grumbled loudly about how messy he is, how forgetful he is, how he is always late. It is a second marriage for both, and they each have grown children from their earlier marriages.

Recently, though, the grumbling has dissipated—for reasons that Eve has only just begun to analyze. About a year ago she left the executive job she had been immersed in and set up a consulting business at home. She wanted more time to write and to indulge in bird-watching. But instead of appreciating scarlet tanagers, she found herself appreciating her husband. "Changing my work life meant I wasn't feeding nearly so many hungry mouths emotionally. There used to be so much of me draining away to other people. I had to marshal my generosity, my limited store of flexibility," Eve says. That has helped tip the glass from half empty to half full. "His finer qualities have more room to blossom when I am not all over him all the time," she explains. "To use a Russian phrase, I am not 'standing over his soul' anymore. So he's able to be more generous, to be more spontaneous, even to remember things—because the stakes are not so high."

This shows up most dramatically when they travel, which both of them love to do, though, typically, in very different ways. Their styles still conflict: he wants to wing it; she wants a game plan. But they have figured out how to work with that, Eve says. "We recognize that I'm going to want to know in advance what we are going to be doing at any given moment of every day," she says. "And he's not going to want that. But we have discovered that it seems to be enough for me to know what the schedule is, and then let go of it. I can say, 'Okay. Let's not go on that boat ride we'd planned; let's check out that bazaar instead.'"

Eve is becoming relaxed enough to enjoy Simon's ability to find weird, offbeat, serendipitous experiences. "He can talk to anybody—and does," she says. "Sometimes it irritates me, and I'm sitting around tapping my toe, but then I remember how many wonderful things have come from this. I've even learned to load him up like a guided missile and send him out. We've ended up hearing about things and going places that would not have happened if we had stayed on my schedule."

So what has changed? "I'm much less anxious. I just look at things differently. When Simon annoys me, I can—sometimes, not always—say to myself, 'That's who he is,'" Eve says. This doesn't spell resignation, she insists. To the contrary, she feels that she has moved on, beyond her irritation at the small stuff. She now appreciates the big stuff.

As in so many of the changes we are undergoing, nature may be playing a role in such accommodations. Eve's acceptance of Simon's laissez-faire behavior may be reinforced, according to some studies, by neurological changes that make some women less inclined—or able—to multitask. These days, she isn't racing impatiently ahead of Simon in the getting-things-done department; sometimes it's Eve who "can only do one thing at a time." As the control freaks among us let go a bit, we, like Eve, learn to appreciate ingredients in our lives that we'd seen before as gumming up the works.

The new hormonal mix that emboldens women to both speak up and let go is working to the advantage of some marriages.

As the level of estrogen in the female body lowers, the testoster-one that's always been there is, as the scientists say, "unmasked," giving us a little boost in willingness to take risks. In men, the amount of testosterone that has been raging through the body since puberty diminishes, making many men less combative and some, like Lucy's husband, more inclined toward nesting. It is as though men and women experience a hormonal conver-gence that opens up new realms of compatibility.

Of course, the research on brains and aging is still far from conclusive, and some of it suggests changes that might be less welcome. But the all-important necessity for creating space between partners—in terms of activities, emotional demands, and dependency—may be enhanced by the onset of a desire for quietude and introspection that complements the feistiness that is fueling the changes we are making. A private comfort zone gives each of us room to grow, room to strut our stuff, room to step back and revise our perspective. As each of the women here discovered, change—in marriage as well as throughout Second Adulthood—happens from the inside out. Once she shifted her own priorities, the marriage began to evolve.

By the same token, in the course of renegotiating new terms of endearment with her husband, each woman came to a new perspective on herself as well as on him. When Lauren came back from Peru, she made three resolutions: "Express yourself, live at your own pace, and experience gratitude." They speak to her own well-being but also to the nature of a marriage that con-tinues to be nurturing. Marriages that endure are about the inti-macy of shared history and the joys of embarking together on a journey of self-discovery and reinvention. What makes these devoted companions unusual is that even if they once were, they are no longer always traveling in the same boat or even heading in the same direction.

THE LESSON: Renegotiating a long-standing marriage is just one part of the overall Second Adulthood recalibration that we are undertaking; if I am changing, we ask ourselves does that mean I have to change my husband? The answer will be influenced by the several streams of self-discovery in our lives: the power of saying no as well as yes, the emergence of new passions and priorities, the willingness to let go of old baggage, and an appreciation of the half-full glass. Shared history and goodwill may provide the baseline for mutual reacquaintance and mutual self-discovery. Or not.

Lesson Nine

You *Do* Know What You Want
to Do with the Rest of Your Life

"I am not a has-been. I'm a will-be."

—Lauren Bacall

From the time they can talk, children are bombarded with the question "What do you want to be when you grow up?" They usually have a ready, if unenthusiastic, answer. "Firefighter." "Inventor." "Dancer." "Giraffe." By the time they are in college, the question becomes simply "What do you want to be?" This time the answers are crisp and career oriented—and much more anxiety ridden. As they move through adulthood, the question gets shorter and more open-ended— "What do you want?" The answers get longer: "To run a company and to run a marathon." "To make lots of money." "To get married and have children." "To get elected to Congress." "To lose weight." But they are still future oriented.

As we stand on the brink of the Fertile Void contemplating the next stage of life, it is only natural to revert to the old question in yet another permutation: "What do I want to do with the rest of my life?" We pose it, fully expecting that there is an answer out there that will conform to the pattern of enumerated hopes and dreams: "Go on a safari and *see* giraffes." "Learn to use the new technology." "Get a job." "Retire." "Get healthy." "Everything on the list of things I always wanted to do, but didn't have time for." This time, though, there is a wrinkle: the answer doesn't lend itself to the future tense.

The Fertile Void is about the struggle to orient ourselves to that change of perspective. Falling weightlessly through the Void, unsure of up and down, untethers us from past and future. Though the past is always present, it moves further into the background. By the same token, the future moves further off and gives way to today's challenges and discoveries. What *is* becomes infinitely more interesting than what may be, especially as it becomes more and more likely that what may be will not be welcome. When you finally feel you have a grip on the rest of your life, it is full of breathless and expansive wonder about where you *are,* not specifics about where you are going.

Jennie* is admittedly a little more breathless and accomplished than most of us, but in her enthusiasm for her life, she is a delicious Horizontal Role Model:

> *I have had my own business for 18 years. Additional adventures in the past 30 years include being a television talk show host, owned and operating wind-surfing business, trekked across the Andes Mountains to Machu Picchu, helicopter hiked in the Bugaboo Mountains in Canada, white water rafted in the Grand Canyon, and went on safari in*

South Africa. Couldn't do some of those things now and delighted that they are part of my younger history. I have five adorable grandsons, a wonderful husband of 40 years, three sons and three daughters-in-law and there is so much more I want to do!!!!!

Maree is in the midst of clarifying some here-and-now priorities. After she cut back to three days a week at work, she had time to "think about a couple of concepts" which, significantly, she explains in the present tense:

Generativity is one—doing good for others beyond just my extended clan.

Risk and Challenge is another—I am actively following up all sorts of hunches, openings of jobs, and such, and being really philosophical whilst also following my intuition much more actively. I am not putting up blockers like "I couldn't go off and leave my husband for three months." He has been really supportive of a couple of possibilities which would take me away from hearth and home. One that looks as if it might happen is to go run a school in a very remote part of Western Australia for a term. The school is largely indigenous students and many of the staff. Despite 30-plus years in education, this would be all new and I am excited and hoping it will come off. Why? Because I want to push out my own personal frontiers and challenge myself whilst also helping.

Learning. I am exploring music—vocal and piano and loving it—I never had the opportunity before. I am also doing courses in creative writing, Italian cooking, cycling as well. I have offered to teach a course as a volunteer at a community college on Financial Literacy.

What I have realized is that I am a busy bee—a bit driven and this is how I am and I'm happy that way—so I need to go on being busy without the stress that used to ruin all the joy. I also feel much freer to roll with the dice— my former need for security and sure things is largely gone.

Those three threads give the warp of the fabric of my emerging second life.

As these two Horizontal Role Models describe the fabric of their emerging lives, it is clear that their answers are not about the *what* of the rest of their lives, but about the *how*. That is both the lesson and the gift of the Fertile Void sojourn. The Journey. The Process. The Quality of Life. These vague terms take on vitality with time. We personalize them.

Thinking more deeply about *how* we want to live forces each of us to intensify her exploration of who she is. It is as though we were zeroing in on an essential character trait or profile that will see us through to the end. The emphasis moves from the deck clearing of "If I am not who I was, only older" to the existential "then who am I?" What do I really believe? What do I mean to say? What are the standards I hold myself to (when no one is watching)? The journey through Second Adulthood becomes a quest for authenticity.

That quest drives much of the behavior we find so bewildering—and so thrilling. All the outrageous acts and experimentation, the discarding and questioning, are ways of trying on different truths about ourselves for size. We are looking for hidden virtues, yes, but we are also ready to acknowledge darker impulses. More than one woman has told me naughtily that she wants to live by Mae West's dictum: "If I am forced to choose between two evils, I prefer to take the one I haven't tried yet."

Such bravado is hard-won for women who have been beholden to imposed roles and expectations for too long. Psychologist James Hillman talks about liberating *character*—what you do when you are alone—from *personality*—the traits you have developed to navigate society, which is why it may take awhile to be truly alone with your authentic self; there are a host of masked interlopers in the way.

The impostor syndrome is one—a cruelly critical self-image that discredits confidence-building experiences. It is the secret certainty that no matter how effective you are professionally, no matter how well you guide your children, no matter how good you look, it is not you who is achieving those successes, but a scripted impersonator who is fooling everyone who thinks well of you. Inside you feel like a fraud: "They don't know that if they ask me about X instead of Y at that meeting, I will make a fool of myself." "I really have no idea what I am doing as a mother." "If they saw what I have managed to hide, they would realize that I am fat and ugly."

An early form of the impostor syndrome is Math Anxiety. This affliction of high school girls was identified by sociologist Sheila Tobias back when many of us were those girls. Good math students would dismiss their accurate answers as "a fluke" or "a lucky guess"; they were sure that they wouldn't be able to get it right the next time—hence the anxiety. No matter how consistent their scores, no matter how much they enjoyed the mind games, many young women—including me—gave up on math, convinced that sooner or later it would become clear that we didn't know what we were doing.

Valerie Young has made a career out of helping grown women break free of the impostor syndrome. Not long ago, when she was in graduate school, she read a 1978 study that, despite being decades old, identified feelings she thought only she was experiencing. "The Impostor Phenomenon Among High Achieving Women" by Pauline Clance and Suzanne Imes focused on the situation of professionally successful women like Young, but the description applies much more widely. The researchers found, Young relates, that "many of their female clients seemed unable to internalize their accomplishments. External proof of intelligence and ability in the form of academic excellence, degrees, recognition, promotions and the like was routinely dismissed. Instead success was attributed to contacts, luck, timing, perseverance, personality or otherwise having 'fooled' others into thinking they were smart and more capable than these women 'knew' themselves to be. Rather than offering assurance, each new achievement and subsequent challenge only served to intensify the ever-present fear" of being found out.

We don't want to be afraid of being found out anymore. Just the opposite. The quest for authenticity is an effort to find out for ourselves who is underneath the expectations and the roles and the false fronts; more than that, we are increasingly confident about the worth of what we uncover about ourselves. "Even though the Fertile Void has been a very frightening place to be," writes Tichrahn, "I feel so high on this new energy."

"I am renewed and reenergized but not to do more or achieve more but to *be* more . . . more of my authentic self," announces

Marylou. Her account of how she is doing that offers an especially insightful analysis of the getting-to-know-me process:

> *My relationships, including the one with myself, have shifted. I care more but attach less. Thus I am more accepting, less judgmental, because I have taken a step back, widening my circle of connection in doing so. I have always been a super extroverted, outward focused, high energy person. Now, after four surgeries in eight years, which forced me to submit to downtime to recover, I have learned to turn inward. The more I accept myself, warts and all, the more I depend less on people and activities to give my life meaning—and the more I find myself falling into contentment.*
>
> *I have become what I once would have called a self-centered slug, caring a great deal about things that aren't really very important perhaps in the big scheme of things— like planting $400 worth of Purple Wave Petunias that provide eye candy for my husband and me—and all who walk past our house. Once I would have felt guilty to not have sent that $400 to Women for Women International or The Heifer Project. . . . My days of hurtling out the door to help my clients, increase community service options, or raise funds for Just Causes are at this point on hiatus. And I am okay with that.*
>
> *It isn't that I don't have energy or concern for causes any more. I do. It isn't that I stopped caring about mental health issues, community well-being, empowering women toward financial stability or feeding AIDS orphans. I do. But I also care about breathing into the moment, taking*

stock of my many blessings, not the least of which is return-
ing to good health, enjoying a loving, passionate relation-
ship with the love of my life, being a good neighbor, and
being awake. Awake to what a wonderful experience life is
despite war, poverty, illness, loss, and pain.

   I now care as much about myself as I do others. As Vic-
toria Beckham would say, "that is major!" I am not angry,
disillusioned, determined to make changes or right wrongs.
I am content to be. I am a 61-year-old woman adapting
to the process of aging, who loves her family and friends
wholeheartedly, who serves in small, perhaps unnoticed,
ways the needs of others and who is delighted and enthralled
with The Way Life Is.

Letting go as Marylou has—of the delusion that it is possible to control life's events, of the demoralizing suspicion that
others have it better or do it better, of the prepackaged "you"—
eliminates false requirements that hold us at bay from our
"warts and all" self. Once face-to-face with our failings, they
usually don't look all that ugly. An e-mail that was circulating
recently sums up the exuberance of judgment-free self-discovery.
Headed "Happy IVGLDSW Day [International Very Good
Looking, Damn Smart Woman's Day]" it urged all VGLDSWs
to carry on. "If you can't be a good example—then you'll just
have to be a horrible warning." It is, quite simply, time to let
yourself off the hook.

   It is also time to let others off the hook. Or at least unhook
their transgressions and cruelties from our psyches. You will
probably never know why so-and-so turned on you thirty years
ago or said that hurtful thing. So what? Maria* had held on

to a righteous grudge since her oldest sister "squeezed" the two other sisters out of their father's estate. When that sister was diagnosed with a degenerative disease, Maria "felt no empathy for her. I felt it was karma and went on with my life. I felt in my heart that it was sweet revenge." Twenty years passed and her son was getting married. The third sister came in for the wedding and caught Maria up on recent developments. The offending sister was, she heard, "doing very poorly, she was a complete invalid, her sons had turned from her, and she had become so bitter. My younger sister was flying up to her [after the wedding], and she asked me if there was anything I wanted to say to her. The first thing that came out of my mouth was 'Tell her what goes around comes around.'" Her own corrosive voice caught Maria by surprise. "At that instant I heard myself, I was ashamed of what I had said. So I turned back to her and handed her some favors from the wedding, a few pictures of my sons and baby grandson, a rose from the centerpiece to be pressed, and said 'Give these to her, tell her I am sorry she was too ill to be able to join in on all the fun, she was in my thoughts and in my prayers.' At that moment I cried, yet I felt a great weight lifted from me."

Dr. Paul Brand, who is a hand surgeon, has a unique perspective on the foulness of harbored resentments. "I'm sometimes called up to operate on someone who has filed suit against the person responsible for his or her injury. I've noticed that many of the patients involved in bitter lawsuits take much longer to heal," he writes. "Their anger at and the desire to punish the person who hurt them seems to enhance the pain," he adds, "and may even interfere with the body's healing mechanism."

The lightness that comes with making peace with who you are and what has happened can literally go to your head. Trading false pride and shoulda-woulda-coulda thinking for authentic inventiveness opens up new realms of self-discovery. For one thing, with the passing of the impostor syndrome the fear of appearing foolish gives way to a delight in *being* foolish. Playing silly games with grandchildren, trying to master tango moves, going for a totally off-the-wall opportunity, building "inappropriate" relationships. What's more, all this is actually good for you. Dr. Vaillant's six points for aging well include this one: "Learning to play and create . . . and learning to gain younger friends as we lose older ones add more to life's enjoyment than retirement income."

The same goes for the clumsiness of trying to regain learning skills and the humiliation of "feeling stupid" in the face of a new body of knowledge. Dr. Andrew Weil describes a patient who was about to give up her efforts to master the computer. "Try to think of kinds of learning that create that kind of intense frustration for you," he advised her. "Then just make yourself do them. You don't have to succeed; it is the effort that increases brain plasticity and flexibility."

Aimless improvising—formerly known as wasting time— may, unexpectedly, lead to the exact opposite: an opportunity for achievement on your own authentic terms. Carole Carson retired from a successful business career at fifty-nine and found herself face-to-face with "the fact" that she would "always be fat." She is five feet one, and at the time she weighed 182 pounds. Since she had nothing better to do, she decided to try to shed those pounds one last time. The reason that every diet she had ever attempted had failed, she decided, was that she always dieted in secret; if others were watching her progress, she might actually stick to it.

So Carole found some playmates. She signed on with a fitness coach and wrote her local newspaper offering to chronicle her efforts to shape up in their pages. Soon she was shedding the weight and hearing from people who were grateful to discover that they were not alone. Eventually she helped organize a "meltdown" in her California county: one thousand people were assigned to small teams that competed for the most weight lost in two months. Together they shed almost 7,600 pounds. Since then she has organized more meltdowns, written a book, and has been working harder than before she retired. "But now," she says, "I'm doing things I really want to do." Nowadays she still has nothing better to do, but this time it is because she can't imagine anything better to be doing.

My favorite highflier is a fifty-one-year-old Swedish woman, Eva Birath, whose life was turned upside down when she was fired from her high-level, high-paying job as a marketing executive. She had to sell her house and her car and was at a complete loss about what to do next. To get through the day, she began going to the local gym. One of the trainers there commented that she had the physique of a bodybuilder. Still with nothing better to do, she signed up for a tournament-training program. After months of a grueling regimen, she began to win contests. Having let go of her former life, her current life started to fill up with bodybuilding and a long-lost passion for painting, which quickly became a source of income. "The hardest part," about her new way of living, Eva says now, "is people's attitudes. You know how you have those circles of people who are your friends? Suddenly I wasn't invited to those parties anymore. I think they thought I was strange. But," she adds, sounding the familiar cry of Second Adulthood, "I don't care!"

If concentrating on the *how* of our lives breaks old behavioral taboos and clears out emotional baggage, it also enlarges our field of potential attachments, a "widening circle of connection," as Marylou put it. Fellow students of all ages. Colleagues at a new job or newly interesting coworkers at the old one. Start-up business partners. Like-minded political rabble-rousers. Distant cousins identified by looking up a family tree. Reconnected friends from the past. At the same time, new frontiers of intergenerational intimacy are opening up. Grandchildren provide unanticipated joy and devotion for many women. Occasionally a daughter-in-law becomes a soul mate. Gerry*, who raised three sons, is forming a delightful bond—somewhere between parent and girlfriend—with the wife of one of her sons. "We talk almost every day," she says. "And not about my son. We talk about our lives."

> *If I'm walking to work I'll call her, or if she's driving home from work she'll call me, just to chat. I totally relate to her. I mean it's clear to me she's of a different generation, but I'm not aware of it, it's just interesting. We talk about the kids a lot because we're both very involved with them.*
>
> *She calls me when she's fed up with my son, and she'll say, you know you're the only person I can tell this to. And I listen, and I can sympathize, I think, "yeah, I know that about him," and I don't get upset or defensive particularly, and then she feels she can tell me because I won't be disloyal to him.*
>
> *We talk about marriage. I've had years of experience, so when there was a time last spring when she and my son*

were fighting a lot, I had a perspective on it. Like how you deal with a husband and children, and how you kind of keep your eye on the fact that, you know how husbands react when they see you totally absorbed with the kids, that kind of stuff. I have a longer view of all of that. I said, "the two of you need to go out and have sex."

It's like with women friends where when you sense a particular kind of affinity with a certain woman you just find you can talk freely to them, you don't have to think about what you're going to say. One of the most endearing, and annoying, qualities of hers is that whatever her mood is, she'll tell you, and that makes her very safe, you know, because she doesn't withhold.

Gerry admits that she probably wouldn't have made herself available to this kind of intimacy at an earlier point in her life. "I think just knowing myself earlier I would have been more closed and more cautious."

Patricia, who is sixty-six and has no children of her own, has discovered the satisfactions of mentoring some of the young people she encounters in her philanthropic work. "I think of mentoring as really listening to the potential of younger people," she says, "and helping them to express their own desires and wisdom, and talking about values that animate one's life and one's work." Those new relationships are her way of being connected with her own past—and their future.

The challenge of mentoring is to not sit back and say, "Well, I have the experience," or, "When I was your age," but really to encourage their insights and then help them build on that, perhaps drawing on my own experience. To take a nonprofessional example, if somebody is deciding whether or not to get married, and I sense a lot of ambivalence, I'll say, "Well you know there really is no hurry." And then I'll tell them a personal story, like about how I was traveling with the man who became my second husband and I realized there was something dramatically wrong with our relationship and we shouldn't get married, but I went through with the wedding, because I was too embarrassed to cancel the caterer. The moral of that story is: go with the gut. Or sometimes I will volunteer in a neutral way, "I have found it very helpful to get professional help. I had a very successful experience in psychotherapy."

What I do is to ask questions—"What do you think about such-and-such?" Or, "I get the sense from your generation that people aren't looking at skin color and sexual preferences. Is that true?" I might say, "I have a lot of trouble with hip-hop music, what is that about? Do you hear that it's misogynous?" That's a question I asked the young man who's working for me, an African American guy. Well then he started talking about what hip-hop means, what rap means. I think that he agreed that it was misogynous. But then he talked about people who are trapped by the culture, and we had a whole conversation. And that sort of led us into a broader kind of serious conversations about politics, about empowerment, about how one deals with issues of race and class.

I find, since I'm the boss, that in a workplace situation some professional distance is helpful. It's a question of boundaries. For instance, if a young woman employee wants a personal relationship with me, I might be disappointed. I can think of one example in which a woman who was quite close to me, working for me—she was a night law student—and then she, in my view, succumbed to the lure of the private sector and is now working in a business context; she really doesn't have the kind of interest that I thought she did. Another young woman just kind of outgrew me; she got busy with other things. She's engaged, she's got a new job. There were no bad feelings. I outgrew some of my mentors. So I think that's in the natural order of things.

I am a child of the '60's. We started out with a lot of idealism, a lot of belief of our ability to make things better in the world, in a variety of ways, whether it was for women or the environment, or poverty or progressive politics or whatever. What I'm seeing now is a lot of younger people, in their late twenties, early thirties, who are seeing that in themselves too; there's a spark that I relate to that I remember from my own early adulthood. I feel it's important to keep that ignited.

For Ethel, who worked so hard at rebuilding her community of friends, the new relationship was one that most women had become familiar with years earlier. Throughout her otherwise very successful and friend-filled life, she had a history of ill-fated romantic attachments. She resigned herself to the "fact" that scars from growing up in a profoundly dysfunctional family would always keep her from forming a loving partnered relationship. So when, in her late forties, she felt the need to evaluate her life, she focused elsewhere—on the way her work had taken over her life and an unfamiliar loneliness. She went into therapy; she reconsidered her priorities; and she began to recalibrate her life—in other words, she plunged into the Fertile Void.

Two years later she was feeling much better about herself. She was enjoying her political work and reconnecting with old friends. Those friends began to do what friends (married friends, anyway) do: they tried to introduce her to men. One day Susan called with an invitation. As Ethel tells it, she didn't make it easy for her friend:

> *"Yom Kippur is coming, I want you to go to shul with me," she said. And I said, "I'm not going to shul, but if I go, I go to the gay and lesbian shul, with my friend, Andy." Then she called me to go with her for the next Jewish holiday. I said to her, "Susan, if you want to see me, let's have lunch, let's have dinner, why are you inviting me to these religious things which you know I'm not that interested in, but more importantly they don't allow us to talk." So she said, "Okay, the reason I was inviting you to shul is because there's someone I want you to meet." I said, "Susan, I don't do this." And she said, "What do you mean you don't do this?" I said, "I don't date, I don't get set up, you know this is my life, this is how it is. I'm fine with it, and I don't want to get confused. If I say yes I'm just going to hyperventilate, freak out." But Susan doesn't ever take no for an answer. Besides, she told me "he's a widower, he's just entering the dating market after like twenty years not dating; he's not looking to get married, and he's a nice guy, he's extremely smart, he loves women, and it's only brunch." I said, "It's only brunch to you!"*

Not surprisingly Ethel canceled the first date they made, but mindful of Susan's persistence, she accepted a second invitation.

From the first moment I met him, I felt like I knew him all my life. He was a mensch. But I never thought this would be romantic; I have a lot of very close male friends, I thought he would just be another one. Then we had a second date where I went over to his house and we watched the returns for the Iowa caucuses. And then on our third date we had this conversation over dinner that was unbelievably honest and intimate, and I fell in love. I just fell in love. And all the things you worry about when you haven't dated as long as I haven't dated—about having sexual intimacy, about being attractive—none of that happened, I mean your body just kind of takes over. I was so comfortable and familiar with him. I was fifty-three and he was fifty-five, and there's a lot of baggage that comes with that. But he made me feel like he really knew who I was—there was not this, "Oh, my God, when he finds out about me." And I really knew who he was.

Being loved for her authentic self has cast the rest of Ethel's life in a new light. She has moved past her old emotional wounds and on to other loving relationships. As her fifty-fifth birthday approached, she found herself overwhelmed with gratitude for her "chosen family" and wanted most of all to "celebrate life." "I had *four* birthday parties. I had a party in New York with fifty something people, and a party in Washington with twenty-five people; I had a party in Chicago with fourteen people, and I had a party in San Francisco with eight people, and in each one I took the time to thank each person with one specific example—I wanted them to know they really made a difference in my life."

Since marriage also brought her financial independence, Ethel has been able to refocus her professional skills—and her gratitude—on what she wants to do with the rest of her life. She had always been active in social justice movements and believed in creative people. Now she is doing pro bono consulting for nonprofits and funding cutting-edge projects. Although the political controversy over Social Security includes the assertion that the older half of the population is a threat to entitlement programs, the truth is that women like Ethel are finding that one of the strongest impulses to come from our inward journey is generosity. Though few of us can afford to give back with a big check, many women are exploring other ways to share the plenitude they are feeling. Our collective potential is beginning to build new options:

The Peace Corps is recruiting us. And we are signing up in record numbers; people over fifty are close to 10 percent of the 7,750 volunteers.

The higher education community is taking note of us. Sociologist Rosabeth Moss Kanter and some colleagues at Harvard Business school have proposed a totally new program—SAIL, the School for Advanced Institutional Leadership—designed to harness and retool the skills of those over fifty who "want to change the world."

Innovative programs, such as Civic Ventures, are promoting a wide range of rewarding opportunities in unpaid, reduced-salary, or paid work. "The goal now," its founder Marc Freedman writes in *The Encore Society,* "is to be able to stop climbing the ladder and start making a difference, to trade money for meaning, to have the latitude to work on things that matter most."

The caregiving crisis is producing organizations, legislation experts, and activists who are making the issue their own. Many of them have firsthand experience with everything from destructive government policy (tax law that actually penalizes rather than supports caregiving) to the lack of safety nets for those who are on duty 24/7. (WomanSage, a West Coast group, raises money to send beleaguered caregivers on a week-long cruise—with full-time nursing service for the patient back home.)

And as our generation of women continues to start businesses at a breathtaking rate, it is noteworthy how many of those businesses are built from our life experiences. Six out of one hundred enterprises selected for microloans from Count Me In for Women's Economic Independence were founded by breast cancer survivors who wanted to help others coping with the disease or with problems they encountered. "Women are natural marketers," notes *Time* magazine's Nancy Gibbs, "even of their worst fears. Their instinct when they get in trouble is to talk about it with other women. So once they have weathered the crisis, they are ready to become crisis managers."

To those who look at what needs to be done and despair of making a difference, the late Anita Roddick, founder of The Body Shop and later-life world changer, had this to say: "If you think you're too small to have an impact, try going to bed with a mosquito."

Our Horizontal Role Models are living the rest of their lives in ways they surely couldn't have anticipated when they first asked themselves what they wanted to do. As the *what* becomes *how,* the questions merge into the answers. The quality of a day or a relationship or a piece of work is what matters. Even more important, the standards for those experiences are set by each of us for herself from her accumulating moments of personal truth. For me, the result is a statement of purpose: I want to be the truest self I can reach. I want to do the best I can toward those I love and expect no more from them. I want to celebrate the gift of the present. With authenticity and gratitude. With curiosity and mastery. With courage and generosity. With humor and empathy. And a grain of salt.

THE LESSON: For every one of us the rest of life is here. What we do with what *is* will become more challenging as we move on through Second Adulthood. How we live each day, whom we build relationships with, what we contribute to the world will bring the satisfactions. Those choices are driven by the ongoing quest for authenticity embodied in the question "Who am I when no one else is looking?"

Lesson Ten

Both Is the New *Either/Or*

*The old woman is never wholly who she thinks she is
because she's also always everyone she ever was—
though never quite the woman others are sure they knew.*

—Robin Morgan, "The New Old Woman"

For my generation of women, life so far has been branded
by responsibilities, objectives, and messages that frequently seemed irreconcilable forces: work and family. Independence and dependence. Fat and thin. Strength
and accommodation. Love and success. Now a new physics is
emerging, although the one-step-forward, one-step-back nature
of our days can obscure the shift. As I survey the cluttered and
untamed terrain of Second Adulthood, the unlikely word *equilibrium* comes to mind. I see women in infinitely diverse circumstances who are experiencing something that eluded us until
now, despite our desperate efforts to straddle multiple roles: a
precarious but real sense of balance. Who would have thought
that given all the turmoil and false starts—all the conflicts and

contradictions—of this stage of life, we would reach a plateau of reconciliation and synthesis?

I am as surprised as anyone to have arrived at a place of peace and contentment. As I wrote this book, I was, in fact, looking for a different dynamic: the widest range of insight and experience I could offer, no matter how off-the-wall, and the reassurance that the existence of so many contradictory approaches would bring. My point was that there is no right way to do Second Adulthood, nor is there any right answer for a given moment in a given woman's life. Inconsistency, I tried to say, is the nature of adventure. Looking back over these pages, I am struck by how often I came upon a "paradox" or an "irony" or an "on the other hand" in my efforts to sort out the forces of good change / bad change, reaching out/ going inward, taking/giving, holding on/ letting go, getting grounded / taking off, and feeling new/ feeling old. Each Life Lesson contains at least one.

> *Yes, you are older chronologically and physiologically, but you are younger in terms of time spent outgrowing who you were before you began figuring out some things.*

> *But it is another of the ironies of this strange new world of ours that while our defiance is directed at seizing control of our lives, the anger that is behind it can make us feel just the opposite: out of control.*

> *Just as we are getting more emotionally and psychologically daring, some of us need to be more careful physically, holding on to stair rails, not running for every bus, switching from the treadmill to the elliptical trainer. Just as we are becoming more*

comfortable with who we are inside, disconcerting external signs of aging can make our appearance unrecognizable and undermine our self-confidence.

Aimless improvising—formerly known as wasting time— may, unexpectedly, lead to the exact opposite: an opportunity for achievement on your own authentic terms.

On the one side is the shedding of excess emotional garbage: the abandonment of lost causes, the downgrading of expectations, and the acceptance of the losses that time brings. On the other side is the letting go that enables us to move beyond those losses. Reduced expectations, for example, free up the imagination for new experiments. Getting through the bad times enables us to take our measure and focus on what really matters going forward.

Even though we keep re-creating familiar patterns (despite our efforts to change some of them), we also feel we are breaking out of old constraints. As much as we long to set goals, we feel more alive when we are reconsidering them. The more we are in flux, the more grounded we feel. The further we get from who we were, the closer we feel we are getting to who we are.

Now, looking back over these dichotomies and ironies, I realize that even as I was enumerating them, they never were discordant, but rather they established a rhythm of their own. Up and down, trial and error, saving and shedding. A seesaw is not a very elegant philosophical model, but it serves here, especially if you consider its fulcrum: the grounded center that supports the highs and lows but doesn't itself get thrown off balance. Seen from that one still point, the contradictory factors in our current lives appear to compensate for one another. You soar, you tumble, but you keep your seat.

The new paradigm is an exercise in both/and. Moving upward and onward, under this system, is less about making choices or making progress than about crafting compromises, de-escalating conflict, and generating momentum. "Wisdom has a purpose," writes Dr. Nuland, "and that purpose is action. This means that action must sometimes be taken with the full understanding that decisions may possibly result in less than perfect consequences. Because taking action in the face of incomplete information is the usual condition in which wisdom needs to be applied." The information any of us has at any given moment is incomplete to say the least—and as we have seen, often contradictory—but the energy, daring, and resilience we are beginning to count on informs our bounces from one "new normal" to the next.

Deb is savoring her moment:

> *Courage comes with age. I would not have been able to do some of the things I do now, even in my forties. Courage and a kind of faith and acceptance, that even if things don't work out, I'm happy to be doing them just the same. I've rediscovered laughter and play, the kind I had when I was a kid. I go out into the woods and talk to the trees. The woods have become my church without walls and my spirituality is thriving. I walk and meditate, go within, getting to know myself on all levels. Like an onion I am peeling*

*back the layers of myself and with each passing year I am
less fearful of new layers. I'm learning my fears won't kill
me; rather, once faced they fade and I feel strong. I keep
moving forward . . .*

*At this point in my life I am facing my fears and heal-
ing the hurts. I know there is no such thing as perfect and I
no longer strive toward unrealistic goals and expectations.
I've learned how to say no and not take any doo-doo from
anyone. I now trust my instincts and set my boundaries and
walk away from people, places and things that are hurtful
or harmful.*

*This acceptance is liberating. . . . It's also a relief to
know what I want and to have the gumption to go after it.
Not much holds me back these days. Fear is replaced with
faith in myself.*

If the Fertile Void is where we are tossed about by confusing
new impulses, in this next stage of Second Adulthood we begin
to consolidate the knowledge, insights, and know-how—the
wisdom—we have salvaged from that wrenching ride. Saying
no and the Fuck-You Fifties teach us not to fear conflict—or
much of anything else, for that matter. Self-confidence leads to
mastery, and authenticity to generosity of spirit. Increasingly
we are able to look contradictions and conflict straight on, find
delight in absurdity, and take people (including ourselves) for
what they are.

As a result, and despite the crises that attend this stage of life,
we don't get thrown as far as we have over much smaller events in
the past. Among the psychologists, physiologists, and philosophers
who are studying aging, *mellowness* has become a technical term

for the midlife plateau of equanimity. (Actually, the word means "maturity" and "ripeness" and "fullness" and "depth" as well as simply "laid-back.") The ability to pick yourself up and move on, to let stuff go, to accept what is and cherish it, to make change and take the consequences, to roll with the punches—that daily resilience pays off in the long term too. "Successfully coping with crises and hardships in life might not only be the hallmark of wise individuals," observes psychologist Monika Ardelt, "but also one of the pathways to wisdom." For the first time for many of us, the word *wisdom* isn't a distant ideal or a ridiculous throwaway, but a quality of mind to look for in ourselves.

In one respect it is already there. In the miraculous adaptations our bodies make to time and circumstance. Scientific findings of compensating physiological forces remind us of the body's exemplary capacity to make the most of change. Neuroscientists are producing new examples every day. As we age, our brains, which have always distributed tasks across more gray matter than the male brain, call upon an even wider range of sites to handle our needs. As a result, writes Dr. Gene D. Cohen, the "increasing use of both sides of the brain for cognitive processes—bilateral brain involvement—can support a more balanced perspective on life that draws on both our logical, analytical powers as well as our nonverbal, intuitive capacities. . . . Compared with younger women, the midlife women in a [Berkeley Institute of Personality and Social Research] study had a stronger sense of personal identity, better self-awareness in social environments, more confidence, more control over events in their lives, and greater productivity."

A "balanced perspective" also shows up in our emotional profile. With age, explains psychologist Laura Carstensen, we "are more likely to experience mixed emotions, happiness and a touch of sadness at the same time. Having mixed emotions helps to regulate emotional states better than extremes of emotion," the mellow mode. That sensitivity to fluctuating emotions, motives, and life experiences explains why we find ourselves letting go of a good/bad, right/wrong way of sizing people up in favor of a more sympathetic appraisal of our flawed fellows. In the absence of such judgmental standards, we find new ways to cherish friendships and family.

When we were first thrust into the confusion of the Fertile Void, we feared that we might be crazy or lazy or selfish; now that we are further along, it is beginning to feel as though we might be, on the contrary, healthy, (spiritually) wealthy, and wise. Either/or thinking served us well during an earlier time when choices were opening up all around us and our lives required split-second decisions. Now options are fewer and less clear-cut. Outcomes are less predictable. It is not surprising that sometimes we find ourselves stuck in place, contemplating an array of not-right choices, or mourning the loss of choice altogether. But the longer we live with impermanence—"after celebrating your children's weddings," one woman told me in a status report on her life, "it is difficult to watch the disintegration of their marriages"—the more we find gratitude replacing bewilderment.

That is certainly where I am right now. When I started out on this journey, and for much of the time until now, I felt like a somewhat incongruous figure. When I turned fifty, I had been married for twenty-five years, but my late-in-life kids were still in grade school. At parent-teacher conferences, I would find myself sitting on a miniature chair seeking parenting advice from a woman half my age, but old enough to be my child's mother. I was out of synch with the other parents too; they were full of drive and ambition on behalf of their children, while I was more laissez-faire. "You know, it really doesn't matter what high school they go to, or what college, for that matter," I told them, based on my long experience in the world. Needless to say, I didn't get many coffee invitations. By the time my kids hit adolescence, I was deep into the adolescence redux of menopause—*that* made for some destabilizing moments. When three out of four members of a family are questioning everything, challenging everyone, and riding powerful hormonal waves, vacations can be challenging, to say the least.

As I began to feel anxious about where I was headed, I wondered who or what—certainly not me—would be in charge of my future. It was as though I didn't fit in there, in my own life, either. Then, on my way to sixty, I thought my career was over. After more than thirty years of busy and exciting work in journalism, I was asked to "step down" (the phrase rings in my ears to this day) as editor in chief of an important magazine. Although I pulled myself together enough to go through the motions of writing a book on contemporary fatherhood, by then I was deep into the Fertile Void. I wrote *Inventing the Rest of Our Lives* to try to figure out what was going on with me. Talking to others—and myself—about what was happening to us and listening to women who were as lost as I was helped a lot. In the course of finding the words and the thinking needed to shed light on our circumstances, I got through the Fertile Void.

I started this book with a much stronger sense of my self. The world around me seemed more manageable, and I felt more at home in my life. No longer obsessed with the question "What do I want to do with the rest of my life," I was getting on with it. As I marveled at my newfound equanimity, the notion of Life Lessons emerged. I began to appreciate how much I, and the women I have been tracking, have learned. About ourselves, but also about the new stage of life we are, as I like to say, "defining by living it."

Looking over the lessons I have identified—so far—I see that I have learned some better than others. I have plenty of homework still to do. For example, I have gotten really good at saying no, and that has been the most galvanizing change for me. I think that has contributed to the rewarding recalibration that has taken place in my marriage. Change itself, has become much less frightening; I have experienced more serendipity and pleasant outcomes than I ever imagined possible when I was trying so desperately to keep everything under control. And, of course, my commitment to my women friends has become deeper, if possible, than ever.

Where I have made less progress is in my efforts to exorcise the Under Toad and replace dread with a more mellow wariness about the "new normal" that some future crisis will bring. I sometimes forget to do unto myself, and I often forget to appreciate the healthy forces inside my thickening body and falling face. All in all, though, my life is adding up nicely. Not as a balance sheet of pluses and minuses, but as a rich and dynamic whole. With good days and bad days, and—most unfamiliar to a drama queen like me—days that are a little of each.

The miracle of now is how our life-long either/or way of seeing the world is morphing into a both/and outlook. The Life Lesson the mellowing process brings is that flux need not be destabilizing. On the contrary, the ebb and flow of our days can induce a sense of peace and contentment, tenderness toward the world, and fullness within ourselves. At any moment, the glass can be simultaneously half full and half empty. And that is okay. Good change and bad change are compatible because change is where the action is. Holding on and letting go is the rhythm of growth. *Yes* and *no* are the passwords to authenticity. Feeling young and old at the same time is the present. More important than options, we are finding joy in the amalgam of experience fragments, the delights of human encounters, the satisfactions of personal effectiveness, and the resilience of our own spirits that make for each of us a life of her very own invention.

Bibliography

AARP Women's Leadership Circle Study, January 2006.

Angelou, Maya. "A Song to Sensuality" from *Even the Stars Look Lonesome*. New York: Random House, 1997.

Angier, Natalie. *Woman: An Intimate Geography*. New York: Anchor Books, 2000.

Barnett, Rosalind, and Caryl Rivers. *Same Difference: How Gender Myths Are Hurting Our Relationships, Our Children, and Our Jobs*. New York: Basic Books, 2004.

Bass, Ellen. *The Human Line*. Washington: Copper Canyon Press, 2007.

Bateson, Mary Catherine. *Composing A Life*. New York: A Plume Book, 1990.

Beauvoir, Simone de. *The Coming of Age*. New York: W.W. Norton & Company, 1972.

Boston Women's Health Book Collective. *Our Bodies, Ourselves for the New Century*. New York: Simon & Schuster, 2005.

Brand, Dr. Paul. *A Doctor's Little Black Book of Remedies and Cures* (self-published).

Brizendine, Dr. Louann. *The Female Brain*. New York: Morgan Road Books, 2006.

Calizar, Yvonne Mokihana. "Nana I Ke Ku . . . Looking to the Source" from *Our Turn, Our Time: Women Truly Coming of Age*. Hillsboro, Oregon: Beyond Words Publishing, Inc., 2000.

Cameron, Julia, *The Artist's Way: A Spiritual Guide to Higher Creativity*. New York: Tarcher/ Penguin, 1992, 2002.

Cohen, Gene D. M.D. *The Mature Mind: The Positive Power of the Aging Brain*. New York: Basic Books, 2005.

Coontz, Stephanie. *Marriage, A History: How Love Conquered Marriage.* New York: Viking, 2005.

Davidson, Sara. *Leap: What Will We Do with the Rest of Our Lives.?* New York: Ballantine, 2007.

Downs, Marion P. *Shut Up and Live! (You Know How): A 93-Year-Old's Guide to Living to a Ripe Old Age.* New York: Avery, 2007.

Dychtwald, Ken. *Age Power: How the 21ˢᵗ Century Will Be Ruled By the New Old.* New York: Jeremy P. Tarcher/ Putnam, 1996.

Freedman, Marc. *Encore: Finding Work That Matters in the Second Half of Life.* New York: PublicAffairs, 2007.

Gilligan, Carol. *In a Different Voice: Psychological Theory and Women's Development.* Cambridge. Harvard University Press, 1993.

——————.*Kyra: A Novel.* New York: Random House, 2008.

Gornick, Vivian. *Fierce Attachments: A Memoir.* New York: Farrar, Straus & Giroux, 1987.

Hall, Stephen S. "The Older-and-Wiser Hypothesis," the *New York Times Magazine,* May 6, 2007.

Healy, Melissa. "Science Is Looking at Women's Innate Need for Friendship," the *Los Angeles Times,* January 15, 2005.

Hillman, James. *The Force of Character and the Lasting Life.* New York: Random House, 1999.

Hoffman, Eileen, M.D. *Our Health, Our Lives: A Revolutionary Approach to Total Health Care for Women.* New York: Pocket Books, 1995.

Jong, Erica. *Fear of Fifty: A Midlife Memoir.* New York: HarperSpotlight, 1995.

Leafe, Diana and Christian Gabriola. *Creating a Life Together: Practical Tools to Grow an Intentional Community.* British Columbia: New Society Publishers, 2003.

Lear, Martha Weinman. *Where Did I Leave My Glasses: The What, When, and Why of Normal Memory Loss.* New York: Grand Central Publishing, 2008.

Legato, Marianne J. *Eve's Rib: The New Science of Gender-Specific Medicine and How It Can Save Your Life.* New York: Harmony Books, 2002.

LeGuin, Ursula K. *Incredible Good Fortune: New Poems.* Boston: Shambala, 2006.

——————. *Sixty Odd.* Boston: Shambala, 1999.

——————. *Tehanu.* Boston: Atheneum, 1990.

Lerner, Harriet. *The Dance of Anger: A Woman's Guide to Changing the Patterns of Intimate Relationships.* New York: Quill, 1997.

Lindbergh, Anne Morrow. *Gift from the Sea.* 50th Anniversary Edition. New York: Pantheon, 1991.

Livingston, Gordon, M.D. *Too Soon Old, Too Late Smart: Thirty True Things You Need to Know Now.* New York: Marlowe & Company, 2004.

Lorde, Audre. *The Cancer Journals.* San Francisco: Aunt Lute Books, 1980.

Macdonald, Barbara, with Cynthia Rich. *Look Me in the Eye: Old Women, Aging, and Ageism.* Midway, FL: Spinsters Ink, 1982, 2001.

Madigan, Tim. *I'm Proud of You: My Friendship with Fred Rogers.* New York: Gotham Books, 2006.

Mead, Margaret. *Male and Female.* New York: William Morrow, 1949.

Morgan, Robin. *A Hot January: Poems 1996–1999.* New York: W.W. Norton & Company, 1999.

——————. *Saturday's Child: A Memoir.* New York: W.W. Norton & Company, 2000.

——————, ed. *Sisterhood is Forever: The Women's Anthology for the New Millennium.* New York: Washington Square Press, 2003.

Northrup, Christiane, M.D. *The Wisdom of Menopause: Creating Physical and Emotional Health and Healing During the Change.* New York: Bantam, 2001.

Nuland, Sherwin B. *How We Die.* New York: Vintage Books, 1995.

——————. *The Art of Aging: A Doctor's Prescription for Well-Being.* New York: Random House, 2007.

Orman, Suze. *Women & Money: Owning the Power to Control Your Destiny.* New York: Spiegel & Grau, 2007.

Paley, Grace. *Fidelity: Poems.* New York: Farrar, Straus & Giroux, 2008.

——————. "Upstaging Time" from *Just As I Thought.* New York: Farrar Straus & Giroux, 1998.

Perls, Frederick S. *Gestalt Therapy Verbatim,* rev. ed. Highland, NY: Gestalt Journal Press, 1992.

Pogrebin, Letty Cottin. *Getting Over Getting Older: An Intimate Journey.* Boston: Little, Brown and Company, 1996.

Propp, Karen, and Jean Trounstine, eds. *Why I'm Still Married: Women Write Their Hearts Out on Love, Loss, Sex, and Who Does the Dishes.* New York: Hudson Street Press, 2006.

Rosen, Ruth. *The World Split Open: How the Modern Women's Movement Changed America.* New York: Viking, 2000.

Rubenfeld, Ilana. *The Listening Hand: Self-Healing Through the Rubenfeld Synergy Method of Talk and Touch.* New York: Bantam Books, 2000.

Rubin, Lillian. *Uncharted Territory: Living the New Longevity.* Boston: Beacon Press, 2007.

Sedlar, Jeri and Rick Miners. *Don't Retire, REWIRE! 5 Steps to Fulfilling Work That Fuels Your Passion, Suits Your Personality, or Fills Your Pocket.* New York: Alpha Books, 2003.

Sewell, Marilyn, ed. *Breaking Free: Women of Spirit at Midlife and Beyond.* Boston: Beacon Press, 2004.

Scheffler, Judith, ed. *Beyond the Corner Office: Essays by Nine Women.* 1st Books Library, 2004.

Schwartz, Pepper. *Prime: Adventures and Advice on Sex, Love, and the Sensual Years.* New York: HarperCollins, 2007.

Sheehy, Gail. *New Passages: Mapping Your Life Across Time.* New York: Ballantine Books, 1995.

Shulman, Alix Kates. *Drinking the Rain.* New York: North Point Press, 1995.

—————. *To Love What Is.* New York: Farrar, Straus & Giroux, 2008.

Steinem, Gloria. *Revolution from Within.* Boston: Little, Brown and company, 1992.

Stephens, Deborah Collins, with Jackie Speier, Michealene Cristini Risley, and Jan Yanehiro. *This is Not the Life I Ordered: 50 Ways to Keep Your Head Above Water When Life Keeps Dragging You Down.* San Francisco: Conari Press, 2007.

Taylor, Shelley E., et al. "Biobehavioral Responses to Stress in Females: Tend-and-Befriend, Not Fight-or-Flight," *Psychological Review* 107, no. 3 (2000).

Thomas, Marlo, and Friends. *The Right Words at the Right Time, Volume 2: Your Turn!* New York: Atria Books, 2006.

Tobias, Sheila. *Overcoming Math Anxiety,* Revised and Expanded. New York: Norton, 1993.

Trafford, Abigail. *My Time: Making the Most of the Rest of Your Life.* New York: Basic Books, 2003.

Transition Network, The and Gail Rentsch. *Smart Women Don't Retire—They Break Free.* New York: Springboard Press, 2008.

Vaillant, George E., M.D. *Aging Well: Surprising Guideposts to a Happier Life from the Landmark Harvard Study of Adult Development.* Boston: Little, Brown and Company, 2002.

Weil, Dr. Andrew. *Healthy Aging: A Lifelong Guide to Your Physical and Spiritual Well-Being.* New York: Alfred A. Knopf, 2005.

Web Sites and Organizations*

AARP
www.aarp.org
The leading organization in the United States for people age fifty and older. Features news, resources, and publications, including the *AARP Bulletin* and *AARP the Magazine*.

Age Beat
www.asaging.org/agebeat/
A free newsletter of the Journalists Exchange on Aging. Features news, updates from the American Society on Aging, and links.

American Association of Homes and Services for the Aging
www.aahsa.org
Features consumer information, fact sheets on aging services, and updates on recent legislation.

---

*While the author has made every effort to provide accurate telephone numbers and Internet addresses at the time of publication, neither the publisher nor the author assumes any responsibility for errors or for changes that occur after publication. Further, the publisher does not have any control over and does not assume any responsibility for author or third-party Web sites or their content.

Assisted Living Federation of America
www.alfa.org
Provides information on finding assisted living communities and learning about long-term care choices. Features publications, resources, and programs, and a store.

Avon
www.avon.com
Empowering women through a range of grant programs and events.

Beacon Hill Village
www.beaconhillvillage.org
Beacon Hill Village helps persons age fifty and older who live on Beacon Hill and in its adjacent neighborhoods in Boston, Massachusetts, enjoy safer, healthier, and more independent lives in their own homes—well connected to a familiar and attentive community. The site provides information on available services, a monthly event calendar, a newsletter, and a link to *The Village Concept: A Founder's Manual* for those wishing to create a similar plan in their neighborhood.

BlogHer
www.blogher.com
The online community for women who blog.

Caregiver Credit Campaign
www.caregivercredit.org
The Caregiver Credit Campaign urges support for all who give care to everyone who needs it, in families of blood or choice, including caring for aging parents; taking responsibility for a disabled, ailing, or dying friend, relative, partner, or spouse; raising children. Strategies for assisting caregivers include converting the child tax credit to a caregiver tax credit, making the credit fully refundable, and increasing its value.

Carole Hyatt Leadership Forum
www.carolehyatt.com
A resource for women embarking on the process of changing careers, changing jobs, becoming entrepreneurs, or reenergizing a career that has stalled.

Catalyst

www.catalyst.org

A nonprofit research and advisory organization working to advance women in business. A leading source of information on women in business for the past four decades, Catalyst has knowledge and tools that help companies recruit, retain, and advance top talent and enable women to reach their potential.

CDC—Healthy Aging

www.cdc.gov/aging/

A U.S. government site addressing health concerns of older adults. Features statistics, links, news, and publications.

Center for the Advancement of Women

www.advancewomen.org

Founded by Faye Wattleton, former president of Planned Parenthood, the center is an institution for research, education, and advocacy on women's issues. Features a monthly newsletter.

Center for Women's Business Research

www.nfwbo.org

Information about women business owners and their enterprises worldwide.

Christiane Northrup, M.D.

www.drnorthrup.com

Features women's health information and news, online journals, and a store.

Civic Ventures

www.civicventures.org

A national nonprofit organization founded to expand the contributions of older Americans to society and to help transform the aging of American society into a source of individual and social renewal. Features publications, projects, grant information, and sources.

Count Me In

www.count-me-in.org

Count Me In for Women's Economic Independence is the leading national not-for-profit provider of online business loans, resources, and community for women entrepreneurs. Features programs, business advice, grants, and an online community.

The Dana Foundation

www.dana.org

A site for brain information. The Dana Press features free publications, *Brain in the News* and *BrainWork*.

Dove Connections

www.dove.us/#/connections/

The blogging site of the Dove Company. Features editorials, blogs, and a lively comments section on topics such as personal growth and self-esteem.

Eileen Fisher, Inc.

www.eileenfisher.com

Grant programs for women-owned businesses and self-image programs for women.

Emily's List

www.emilyslist.org

One of the nation's largest political networks and the largest financial resource for women candidates. EMILY's List's WOMEN VOTE! program helps elect Democrats up and down the ballot. Features news, programs, and job/volunteer information.

Encore: Work That Matters in the Second Half of Life

www.encore.org

A community site from Civic Ventures that provides news, resources, and connections for individuals and organizations establishing "encore careers" that combine social contribution, personal meaning, and financial security.

Families and Work Institute
www.familiesandwork.org
Founded in 1989, Families and Work Institute is a nonprofit center for research that provides data to inform decision making on the changing workforce, changing family, and changing community. The institute offers some of the most comprehensive research on the U.S. workforce available.

Foundation for Women's Wellness
www.thefww.org
A small nonprofit public charity dedicated to medical research and education of critical women's health issues. Established in 1997 by Dr. Lila Nachtigall, an internationally renowned physician recognized for her work in women's health and hormones, FWW is guided by knowledgeable physicians, researchers, and private sector specialists.

Institute for Women's Policy Research
www.iwpr.org
The institute conducts research and disseminates its findings to address the needs of women, promote public dialogue, and strengthen families, communities, and societies, specifically in the area of economics and public policy. The site features resource links, publications, and conference information.

International Longevity Center
www.ilcusa.org
A nonprofit, nonpartisan, international research, policy, and education organization formed to educate individuals on how to live longer and better and to advise society on how to maximize the benefits of today's age boom. Conducts a variety of public policy research, scientific consensus workshops, and educational programs.

iVillage, Inc.
www.ivillage.com
The number one destination for women online, dedicated to connecting women at every stage of their lives. iVillage Cares initiative connects women around the world to one another to effect change.

Kaiser Family Foundation
www.kff.org
A private nonprofit foundation focusing on the major health-care issues facing the nation. Features extensive studies, reports, and policy information.

The Kinsey Institute
www.kinseyinstitute.org
Promotes interdisciplinary research and scholarship in the fields of human sexuality, gender, and reproduction. Features publications, library, research programs, and resources.

Lauren Hutton's Good Stuff
www.laurenhutton.com
An online store with Lauren Hutton's makeup line; geared toward women, not girls.

Liz Claiborne, Inc.
www.lizclairborneinc.com
The Liz Claiborne Foundation, established in 1981, supports nonprofit groups that address women's concerns—economic self-sufficiency, family violence, and positive programming for girls.

MedlinePlus: Drugs, Supplements, and Herbal Information
http://www.nlm.nih.gov/medlineplus/druginformation.html
Detailed information on drugs, herbs, and supplements, including their interactions. Can be searched by drug or herb/supplement. A service of the U.S. National Library of Medicine and the National Institutes of Health.

Menopause Magic
www.menopausemagic.org
A New York-based site created by Dr. Patricia Yarberry Allen, an obstetrician and gynecologist at the New York Hospital-Cornell Medical Center. The site is the link for the New York Menopause Center. Also has links to the New York Menopause Research Foundation, Menopause Mentors, and articles.

More Magazine

www.more.com

The online presence of *More* magazine, celebrating women over forty. Features current and past articles, a newsletter, and Suzanne Braun Levine's *Inventing the Rest of My Life* blog.

Ms. Foundation for Women, Inc.

www.ms.foundation.org

The first and leading women's fund and foundation engaged across the United States to build women's collective power to ignite change.

Ms. Magazine

www.msmagazine.com

Launched in 1971, it became a major voice of the women's movement. It still covers women's issues and provides information on women's rights around the world.

National Council for Research on Women

www.ncrw.org

A network of more than one hundred research, advocacy, and policy centers devoted to informed debate on women's issues, including global initiatives.

National Women's Health Network

www.nwhn.org

The National Women's Health Network develops and promotes a critical analysis of health issues in order to affect policy and support consumer decision making. The network aspires to a health-care system that is guided by social justice and reflects the needs of diverse women.

Nia

www.nianow.com

A technique of body-mind-spirit based on the philosophy "through movement we find health."

North American Menopause Society

www.menopause.org

The leading nonprofit scientific organization devoted to promoting women's health and quality of life through an understanding of menopause. This site contains information on menopause, perimenopause, early menopause, menopause symptoms, and long-term health effects of estrogen loss, and a wide variety of strategies and therapies to enhance health.

Oasis

www.oasisnet.org

A national nonprofit educational organization designed to enhance the quality of life for mature adults. Offers programs in the arts, humanities, wellness, technology, and volunteer service.

Older Women's League

www.owl-national.org

The only national grassroots member organization to focus solely on issues unique to women as they age, OWL strives to improve the status and quality of life for midlife and older women. The site has health and retirement information, news, a store, and links to local chapters.

Outward Bound

www.outwardboundwilderness.org

Outward Bound USA's official Web site. Look under "Special Focus Courses" for women-only programs. Outward Bound also has international programs in more than twenty countries. Visit Outward Bound International at www.outwardbound.net.

Peace Corps 50+ Volunteers

www.peacecorps.gov/minisite/50plus/index.cfm

The minisite for adults age fifty-plus who are interested in joining the Peace Corps. Features detailed health-care and insurance information and an application.

Persimmon Tree

www.persimmontree.org

Persimmon Tree, an online literary magazine, is a showcase for the creativity and talent of women over sixty. Features fiction, nonfiction, poetry, theater, and art. Free online subscription available.

The Purpose Prize

www.purposeprize.org

An initiative from Civic Ventures to invest in social innovators over sixty by recognizing outstanding achievements, creating a network of people wanting to use their retirement years for the greater good, and channeling funds and assistance to these new pioneers. Awards five $100,000 prizes each year.

Red Hat Society

www.redhatsociety.com

The worldwide social phenomenon for celebrating women over fifty. More than twenty thousand chapters. Features news, a link, and convention information.

Retirement or WHAT NEXT?

www.retirementorwhatnext.com

Transitions for women over fifty who want to make the most of life and wish to redefine work, consider the possibilities, express creativity, and ponder what's next. Provides workshops, discussion groups, and individual consultations.

Revlon

www.revlon.com

Corporate leader in the fight against women's cancers.

SeniorNet

www.seniornet.org

A nonprofit organization of computer-using adults age fifty and older. SeniorNet's mission is to provide older adults education for and access to computer technologies to enhance their lives and enable them to share their knowledge and wisdom. The site features Web courses, a learning center, research papers and studies, news, and an online community forum where all individuals fifty and older, whether or not they are members of SeniorNet, are welcome to participate in online communities and hundreds of discussion topics.

Seniors for Living

www.seniorsforliving.com

A source for senior housing news and resources for the United States, whether assisted living, independent living, Alzheimer's care, continuing care, retirement living or home care. Features articles about senior housing and senior care, housing type comparisons, free cost worksheet, and a newsletter.

Smith College Ada Comstock Scholars Program
www.smith.edu/admission/ada.php
Established in 1975, this program at Smith College enables women of
nontraditional college age to complete a bachelor of arts degree at a realistic pace, either part time or full time. The program combines the rigorous
academic challenges of Smith with flexibility for women beyond the traditional college age by providing options for reduced course loads, special
academic advising, career counseling, and diverse housing options.

Suze Orman
www.suzeorman.com
Information about Suze Orman's books, television program, contact information, and other resources.

The Transition Network
www.thetransitionnetwork.org
Network that provides a national community for women over fifty as they
move from their career to whatever is next. The network helps women
discover new opportunities, new perspectives, and new ways to make
an impact. Features group volunteer projects, a monthly newsletter, and
resources.

University of Michigan Health System
http://www.med.umich.edu/1libr/aha/umherb01.htm
Basic list of herb-drug interactions. This information is approved and/or
reviewed by U. of M. health system providers.

U.S. Census Bureau
www.census.gov
Resource for publications and reports from the Census Bureau with population, housing, economic, and geographic data.

Wellesley Centers for Women
www.wcwonline.org
WCW is the nation's largest women's research center. Features publications,
news, analysis, and resources.

When Work Works

www.whenworkworks.org

A project of the Families and Work Institute on workplace effectiveness and workplace flexibility. As part of the nationwide initiative, the Web site has resources and information for employers, managers, employees, and the public at large.

The White House Project

www.thewhitehouseproject.org

A nonpartisan organization that promotes women's civic engagement, specifically by working to fill the "leadership pipeline" all the way to the top with diverse and qualified women.

WomanSage

www.womansage.com

A nonprofit membership organization dedicated to educating, empowering, and fostering mentoring relationships among women at midlife. Features a news-based Web site, a quarterly journal, annual conferences, monthly salon meetings, and a network of special interest groups. Chapters in California and Connecticut.

Women's Sports Foundation

http://www.womenssportsfoundation.org/

Founded in 1974 by Billie Jean King, it promotes gender equity in women's sports.

Women@Work Network

www.womenatworknetwork.com

A nationwide network and forum that helps current and returning professional women find work that fits their current life stage. Features a job board, links, and news.

Women's Campaign Forum

www.wcfonline.org

A nonpartisan pro-choice national membership organization dedicated to ensuring women become leaders in public life. Features candidate resources, volunteer opportunities, and more.

Women's eNews

www.womensenews.org

An independent news agency covering issues of particular concern to women and providing women's perspectives on public policy. Subscribe for free and receive daily news stories or daily news summaries and/or a weekly summary.

Women's Institute for Financial Education

www.wife.org

A nonprofit organization dedicated to providing financial education to women in their quest for financial independence. Features articles, links, and a newsletter.

Women's Media Center

www.womensmediacenter.com

An advocacy site dedicated to amplifying progressive women's voices through the media, specifically around the theme of "Women as Leaders and Peacemakers." Features daily news briefs, resources, a library, volunteer opportunities, and a forum.

The Woodhull Institute

www.woodhull.org

Provides ethical leadership training and professional development for women.

Yankelovich

www.yankelovich.com

A consultancy providing information, database, and custom marketing services. The site features information for businesses, including the *Yankelovich Monitor.*

Index

AARP, 54, 122
adolescence, 33, 46, 158, 187
  aging and, 2, 12, 20, 127
  friendships and, 81–83
  legacy of limitations and, 12–13
adventure, 87, 181
  change and, 23, 28, 30
  friendships and, 73, 78
  rest of your life and, 161–62
age, aging, ageism, 1–16, 18–21,
    181–88
  admitting to, 7–8
  balance and, 6–7, 185–86
  benefits of, 2–4
  birthdays and, 6–8, 16, 19, 21, 55
  body and, 1–3, 9, 11–13, 19–20, 26,
    125–44, 181–82, 185, 188
  change and, 1–5, 9, 11, 14, 25–26, 34,
    125–44, 185
  crises and, 99
  expectations in, 12, 130
  Fertile Void and, 14–16, 20–21
  friendships and, 6–7, 10, 66, 69–70,
    75–77, 83, 129
  Horizontal Role Models and, 10–11, 14,
    18–20
  internalization of, 4
  lessons on, 21, 143–44
  marriages and, 12–13, 145–46, 158
  rest of your life and, 163, 167, 169,
    171–73
  saying no and, 46–47, 51, 54–56

  self and, 112–14, 117, 122, 126, 128, 132,
    136, 167
  Serenity Prayer and, 129–30
Aging Well (Vaillant), 143, 145
American Sociological Review, 74
Angelou, Maya, 131–32, 143
anger, 167–68, 181
  friendships and, 65–66
  saying no and, 52–53, 62, 152
anxiety, 157, 160, 164–65, 187
  crises and, 90, 100
  friendships and, 84
appearance, 180
  aging and, 3, 7, 19, 83, 125–26, 128–29,
    132, 188
  rest of your life and, 164, 169–70, 176
Ardelt, Monika, 185
Art of Aging, The (Nuland), 1
assertiveness, 61–62, 109–11, 151
Auchincloss, Sarah S., 92, 94–95, 99, 102–3
authenticity, 182, 184, 189
  change and, 35
  Fertile Void and, 18
  friendships and, 84
  renegotiating marriages and, 146
  rest of your life and, 163–66, 169, 176, 179
  saying no and, 61

Bacall, Lauren, 160
bag lady syndrome, 119
balance, 136, 180–81, 183, 188
  aging and, 6–7, 185–86

Bateson, Mary Catherine, 108
Birath, Eva, 170–71
birthdays, 91, 146
    aging and, 6–8, 16, 19, 21, 55
    change and, 36–37
    crises and, 96–97
    friendships and, 71
    rest of your life and, 176–77
body, 51, 89, 176
    aging and, 1–3, 9, 11–13, 19–20, 26,
        125–44, 181–82, 185, 188
    balance between mind and, 136
    and care of self, 106, 111, 126
    change and, 26, 125–28, 144
    connection between soul and, 135, 144
    friendships and, 70, 74, 78–80
    Horizontal Role Models and, 11, 19–20
    maintenance of, 128–29, 131–32, 136,
        144
Bolen, Jean Shinoda, 101
brain, 80, 169
    aging and, 1–2, 7–8, 14, 126–27, 131, 185
    anger and, 52–53
    balance between body and, 136
    renegotiating marriages and, 158
Brand, Paul, 168
Brizendine, Louann, 52–53, 111

Calizar, Yvonne Mokihana, 84
cancer:
    breast, 3, 87, 91–92, 101, 178
    crises and, 85, 87, 91–92, 95–96, 101–2
    Horizontal Role Models and, 10–11
Cancer Journals, The (Lorde), 101–2
caregiving crisis, 178
Carson, Carole, 169–70
Carstensen, Laura, 185–86
change, changes, 21–41, 53, 125–52, 167
    advice on, 29–36
    aging and, 1–5, 9, 11, 14, 25–26, 34,
        125–44, 185
    crises and, 85
    dichotomies, ironies and, 181–82
    Fertile Void and, 18, 21–22, 27, 29
    friendships and, 67–68, 75–78
    Horizontal Role Models and, 11, 14, 29
    marriages and, 31, 146–52, 154, 157–59
    rest of your life and, 161, 178
    saying no and, 56, 58–61, 188
    self and, 34–36, 115
Change, The (Greer), 91

childhood, children, 5–6, 17, 90, 145–46,
        183, 186–87
    aging and, 6, 9, 11–13, 19
    and care of self, 104–7, 111–13, 117, 119,
        123
    change and, 27–29, 35–37, 40
    crises and, 86, 89, 94–96, 98, 101, 123
    friendships and, 63–65, 67–68, 71,
        73–74, 76–78, 81–83, 98
    Horizontal Role Models and, 10–11
    renegotiating marriages and, 146,
        148–51, 153–56
    rest of your life and, 160, 162, 168–69,
        171–72
    saying no and, 44–47, 58–59
Civic Ventures, 177–78
Clauser, Marge, 12–13, 19
Clinton, Hillary and Bill, 147
Cohen, Gene D., 185
commitment, 61, 149
    anger and, 53
    friendships and, 65, 84, 188
    saying no and, 57–58
community, 26
    and care of self, 111, 113–14, 116–18, 120
    friendships and, 66–70, 75, 174
Composing a Life (Bateson), 108
confidence, 44, 51, 184–85
    aging and, 126, 182
    and care of self, 105, 109–10, 120, 165
    crises and, 89, 95
    friendships and, 66, 78
    rest of your life and, 164–65
consumer industry, 54–55
Cooper, Sue Ellen, 55
coping, 85, 87, 91–92, 103, 178, 185
Cosentino, Nancy, 139–40
courage, 129, 152, 179, 183
    crises and, 89, 91
    friendships and, 81, 84
    saying no and, 42, 48
creativity, 20, 32, 127, 169
crises, 76, 85–103, 178, 184–85
    coping and, 85, 87, 91–92, 103, 185
    friendships and, 81, 85–86, 88, 93–95,
        98–99
    improvising and, 85, 88–89
    lesson on, 103
    marriages and, 87–88, 95, 97, 101, 154
    new normal after, 87–89, 91–94, 97–103,
        188

self and, 101–3, 105, 123
support and, 92–95, 103

Dalai Lama, 123
daring, 18–19, 44
death, 40
   aging and, 2–3, 7, 12–13
   crises and, 85, 91, 96–97, 123
   friendships and, 63, 66, 73, 76–77, 85
   new normal after, 91–92
   of parents, 12–13, 63, 85, 91, 97
   saying no and, 51, 59
Death of a Salesman (Miller), 59
decision making, 183, 186
   and care of self, 105, 111–12, 118, 120
   crises and, 95–97, 100–101
   friendships and, 76, 81
   renegotiating marriages and, 149
   rest of your life and, 169–70, 173
   saying no and, 48, 57–58
dementia, 80, 96, 98, 112
depression, 91, 130
diabetes, 130, 141
divorce:
   and care of self, 105–6, 116
   change and, 35
   friendships and, 73, 76, 83
   new normal after, 91–95, 99–101
   renegotiating marriages and, 148,
      153–54
   saying no and, 45, 48–49
Don't Retire, REWIRE! (Sedlar and
   Miners), 118
Dove pro-aging ad campaign, 69–70
Dunn, Mary Maples, 5–6

education, 143, 186–87
   aging and, 7, 12–13
   and care of self, 105, 107, 110
   change and, 24, 35
   crises and, 88, 95, 100
   Fertile Void and, 15
   friendships and, 68–69, 72, 77, 83
   gender discrimination and, 5–6
   renegotiating marriages and, 149, 152
   rest of your life and, 162–63, 165, 171,
      174, 177
   saying no and, 43–44, 46–47
either/or thinking, 186, 188
Emily's List, 110
employment, 2–5, 136, 180, 187

aging and, 2, 4–5, 7, 9–11, 14
and care of self, 104–5, 109–10, 113–20,
   122
change and, 23–25, 27–28, 31, 36–38, 115
crises and, 85–88, 96–101
Fertile Void and, 16–17
friendships and, 63, 66, 68, 71–72, 74,
   77, 174–75
gender discrimination and, 4, 43, 54, 99
looking for, 24, 31, 99–100, 122
in new normal, 87, 97–101
renegotiating marriages and, 146,
   149–56
rest of your life and, 160–62, 164–65,
   169–75, 177–78
saying no and, 45–48, 51, 54, 58–61
empowerment, 166, 173
   anger and, 53
   and care of self, 123–24
   friendships and, 69, 81
   Horizontal Role Models and, 18
   saying no and, 45, 55, 58
   sexuality and, 138
Epictetus, 61
estrogen, 52–53, 137–38, 158
exercise, 51, 143, 149–51
   aging of body and, 126–27
   and care of self, 106, 111, 113
   change and, 31–32
   Fertile Void and, 15–16
   friendships and, 68, 72
   renegotiating marriages and, 150–51
   rest of your life and, 162–63
expectations, 104, 136, 182, 184
   in aging, 12, 130
   change and, 23, 26–27
   crises and, 87, 91, 94–95, 103
   Fertile Void and, 18, 27
   friendships and, 81
   rest of your life and, 161, 164–65, 169
   saying no and, 45, 52, 58

family, 26, 76, 80, 90, 180
   aging and, 14
   balance and, 186
   and care of self, 107–8, 112–14,
      122–23, 167
   change and, 35–37
   crises and, 85–86, 95, 97–98
   friendships and, 64, 70, 84
   renegotiating marriages and, 151

family *(cont.)*
    rest of your life and, 167–68, 171–72,
        174–76
    saying no and, 45, 48, 59, 61
Faust, Drew Gilpin, 5–7
fear, 184, 186, 188
    aging and, 7
    change and, 29–30, 33, 41
    crises and, 89–91, 100–102
    friendships and, 65, 81, 84
    heart attack symptoms and, 133–34
    renegotiating marriages and, 152
    rest of your life and, 164–65, 169
    saying no and, 42–43, 48–49, 54
Fear of Fifty (Jong), 53
Female Brain, The (Brizendine), 52–53
Fertile Void, 14–21, 184, 186–87
    authenticity and, 18
    change and, 18, 21–22, 27, 29
    Horizontal Role Models and, 16–21
    letting go and, 17–18
    mastery and, 18
    peacefulness and, 17–18, 20
    and recalibrating our place in world, 17
    rest of your life and, 160–61, 163, 165, 175
    time in, 15–17
finances, 166, 169
    advice on, 121–23
    aging and, 13, 128
    and care of self, 105, 109–10, 112–13,
        115–16, 118–23
    change and, 28–31
    crises and, 86, 95, 98–101
    fears and, 29–30, 43
    hang-ups about, 119–20
    renegotiating marriages and, 152–53
    rest of your life and, 160, 170, 177
    saying no and, 43–44, 52
flexibility, 34, 156, 169
Frank, Charlotte, 116–18
Freedman, Marc, 177–78
friendships, 63–86, 133, 145–46, 186, 188
    aging and, 6–7, 10, 66, 69–70, 75–77,
        83, 129
    and care of self, 108–9, 114, 116–17, 122,
        167
    change and, 67–68, 75–78
    circle of trust, 66, 70–71, 74–76, 81
    crises and, 81, 85–86, 88, 93–95, 98–99
    criteria for, 78
    deaths and, 63, 66, 73, 76–77, 85

demystification of, 78–79
Fertile Void and, 15–17
growth of, 81–84
Horizontal Role Models and, 64, 75–78
marriages and, 64, 67, 75–76, 81, 146,
    149–50
medical information exchange and, 141
new, 67–69, 71, 75, 82, 84
nurturing nature of, 74
and opportunities to connect, 72–73
renewal of, 66–68, 72, 75, 171, 175
rest of your life and, 167, 170–72, 174–77
romances and, 174–76
saying no and, 61
statistics on, 74–75
stress and, 79–80, 84
support and, 116–17, 122
unsatisfactory, 71–72
Fuck-You Fifties, 18, 44, 53–54, 56–57, 84,
    110, 137, 184

gambling addiction, 28–29
gardening, 32, 38–39, 166
Garland, Judy, 35
gender differences:
    aging of body and, 131–32
    anger and, 52–53
    and care of self, 108, 120
    friendships and, 75, 79–81
gender discrimination, 4–6, 43, 99
    saying no and, 54–55
generosity, 184
    and care of self, 108, 121, 124
    change and, 36
    friendships and, 75
    renegotiating marriages and, 156
    rest of your life and, 177, 179
Gibbs, Nancy, 178
Gift from the Sea (Lindbergh), 28–29
goals, 182, 184
    and care of self, 117–18
    change and, 27
    Fertile Void and, 15, 20
    renegotiating marriages and, 149
    rest of your life and, 177–78
    saying no and, 61
Greer, Germaine, 91
grudges, 167–69

Halamka, John D., 141
Heading South, 138

Healy, Melissa, 78–80
heart disease, heart attacks, 51, 85
   aging of body and, 130, 132–35, 141–42
   friendships and, 79–80
   symptoms of, 132–34
Hillman, James, 164
Hoffman, Eileen, 142–43
Hofmann, Regan, 139
Horizontal Role Models, 10–11, 13–14, 110, 141–42
   change and, 11, 14, 29
   crises and, 99–102
   Fertile Void and, 16–21
   friendships and, 64, 75–78
   rest of your life and, 161–63, 178–79
   saying no and, 49
   sexuality and, 137
hormones, 51–53, 187
   aging and, 14, 19–20, 137–38
   anger and, 52–53
   and care of self, 111, 113
   friendships and, 79–80
   renegotiating marriages and, 157–58
   sexuality and, 137–38
housework, 150, 152–53
humor, 116, 179
   aging of body and, 130–31
   crises and, 103
Hyatt, Carole, 31

illness, 3, 10–11, 57–59
   aging and, 125, 129–30, 132–36, 139–43
   and care of self, 105, 107, 112–13, 115–18, 120, 123, 166–67
   change and, 37
   crises and, 85, 87–88, 91–92, 95–96, 98, 101–2
   friendships and, 79–80
   medical information exchange and, 141–43
   in new normal, 87–88, 91–92, 101
   renegotiating marriages and, 153
   rest of your life and, 166–68, 178
   saying no and, 51, 58–59
impostor syndrome, 164–65, 169
I'm Proud of You (Madigan), 74
improvising, 116, 169, 182
   crises and, 85, 88–89
   renegotiating marriages and, 156
Internet, 92–93, 142
   and care of self, 110, 113, 167

friendships and, 63–64, 70, 72–73
   saying no and, 42, 49
Inventing the Rest of Our Lives (Levine), 7–8, 187
Irving, John, 90

Jewelia, 72–73
Jong, Erica, 53
journaling, 33–34, 77

Kanter, Rosabeth Moss, 177–79

learning, 14, 109, 184, 188
   aging and, 2, 132
   change and, 27
   crises and, 102
   friendships and, 65–68, 76
   renegotiating marriages and, 157
   rest of your life and, 161–63, 166, 169
   saying no and, 43, 58, 60–61
Le Guin, Ursula K., 22, 36
L'Engle, Madeleine, 2
Lennon, John, 85
lifestyles, 115
   aging of body and, 129
   change and, 31
   friendships and, 75–76
Lindbergh, Anne Morrow, 28–29
listening, 14, 106, 171, 187
   aging of body and, 132
   change and, 33–34
   friendships and, 73–74, 82
   renegotiating marriages and, 155
Livingston, Gordon, 27, 136
longevity, 5, 7, 79, 81
Lorde, Audre, 101–2

MacArthur Foundation Study of Aging in America, 51
Madigan, Tim, 74
marriage, 4–6, 53–54, 145–60, 186
   aging and, 12–13, 145–46, 158
   and care of self, 105–6, 108
   change and, 31, 146–52, 154, 157–59
   crises and, 87–88, 95, 97, 101, 154
   every five years assessments of, 153–54
   friendships and, 64, 67, 75–76, 81, 146, 149–50
   gender discrimination and, 4–5
   mission statement for, 149–50
   renegotiation of, 145–59

marriage *(cont.)*
  rest of your life and, 160, 168, 171–73, 175–77
  saying no and, 45, 49, 54, 56, 58–59, 152, 159, 188
  vows in, 149, 151
mastectomies, 91–92, 141
mastery, 123, 184
  aging of body and, 126
  crises and, 89
  Fertile Void and, 18
math anxiety, 164–65
Mead, Margaret, 109, 126
medications, 30, 130, 140–42
  aging and, 3, 14
mellowness, 184–86, 188
menopause, 14, 48, 89, 109, 187
  aging and, 9, 126, 141
  anger and, 53
  and care of self, 111
  sexuality and, 137, 140
mentoring, 110
  change and, 36
  friendships and, 77
  rest of your life and, 172–74
Miners, Rick, 118
Mirren, Helen, 3–4
Moore, Marianne, 35
More, 3, 8, 54, 110
Morgan, Robin, 56, 180
motherhood, 5, 53, 142
  aging and, 11–14, 19
  and care of self, 107, 122
  change and, 28–29, 34
  crises and, 85, 88, 90–91, 96–98
  deaths of, 13, 85, 91, 97
  friendships and, 64–66, 68, 74, 76–77
  Horizontal Role Models and, 11, 19
  saying no and, 44, 46–47
Ms., 137
multitasking, 15, 51, 157

"Nana I Ke Ku . . . Looking to the Source" (Calizar), 84
Neubauer, Ruth, 69
new normal, 91–95, 183–84
  after crises, 87–89, 91–94, 97–103, 188
  lesson on, 103
"New Old Woman, The" (Morgan), 180
no, saying, 42–62, 184
  anecdotes on, 43–50

  canceling appointments and, 57–58
  in destructive relationships, 49–51
  learning and, 43, 58, 60–61
  lesson on, 61–62
  marriages and, 45, 49, 54, 56, 58–59, 152, 159, 188
  nurturing nature of, 56–57
  stress and, 51–52, 59–60
Northop, Peggy, 54
Nuland, Sherwin B., 1, 126, 128, 130, 132, 183
nursing homes, 98, 113

Onassis, Jacqueline Kennedy, 46
Orman, Suze, 120–21
Our Health, Our Lives (Hoffman), 142–43
oxytocin, 111
  anger and, 52–53
  friendships and, 79–80

Paley, Grace, 10
parenthood, 142, 145–46, 186–87
  aging and, 7–8, 11–14, 19
  and care of self, 104, 107, 112–14, 119, 122
  crises and, 85, 88, 90–91, 94, 96–98
  deaths of, 12–13, 63, 85, 91, 97
  friendships and, 63–66, 68, 74, 76–77
  renegotiating marriages and, 146, 150–51, 155
  saying no and, 44, 46–47
Perls, Fritz, 90–91
planning, 59, 85
  and care of self, 114–15, 118, 121–23
  change and, 31–32, 40
  renegotiating marriages and, 154–56
politics, 4, 10, 26, 58, 99
  and care of self, 109–10, 114
  change and, 30, 35
  friendships and, 66, 71, 77–78, 176
  rest of your life and, 160, 171, 173–78
POZ, 139–40
problem solving, 141, 153
  and care of self, 111, 116, 118
  crises and, 92–93
  friendships and, 79, 81, 84

race, racism, 5, 173
Red Hat Society, 55–56
Reiki, 82–83
relationships, 17, 58–60, 135–36, 139–41
  aging and, 2, 5, 9, 11, 135

and care of self, 105–6, 109, 113, 121–22, 166–67
   change and, 24–25, 27, 30
   crises and, 94, 98–99, 101
   destructive, 49–51
   intergenerational intimacy and, 171–72
   rest of your life and, 166–67, 169, 171–77, 179
   saying no and, 49–51, 58
   sexuality and, 139–40
   see also friendships; marriage
responsibilities, 45, 64, 180
   aging of body and, 129, 136
   and care of self, 108, 123–24
rest of your life:
   change and, 161, 178
   friendships and, 167, 170–72, 174–77
   grudges and, 167–69
   impostor syndrome and, 164–65
   intergenerational intimacy and, 171–72
   lesson on, 179
   mentoring and, 172–74
   new options and, 177–79
   prioritizing and, 162–63, 175
   self and, 164–67, 169, 176, 179
   what to do with, 160–79, 187–88
retirement, 47, 150
   and care of self, 113–14, 116, 118–19, 122
   crises and, 87–88
   rest of your life and, 161, 169–70
   savings for, 113, 119
   sexuality and, 140–41
   understanding consequences of, 118–19
Revolution from Within (Steinem), 3
Right Words at the Right Time, The (Thomas), 28–29
risk, 18, 109, 162
   aging of body and, 130
   change and, 24, 30–31, 40–41
   crises and, 89
   friendships and, 65, 81, 84
   heart disease and, 51
   renegotiating marriages and, 158
   sexuality and, 137, 139–40
Risley, Michealene Cristini, 107
Roddick, Anita, 178
Rogers, Fred, 74
Rubin, Lillian, 112

safety nets, 115, 121, 178
Sebelius, Kathleen, 110

Second Adulthood, 1–2, 7, 9, 11, 13–14, 179–81, 184
   aging of body and, 127, 129, 136
   and care of self, 110, 116, 119
   change and, 22
   crises and, 85, 99
   Fertile Void and, 14, 20
   friendships and, 69
   renegotiating marriages and, 158–59
   rest of your life and, 163, 171, 179
   saying no and, 45, 61
Sedlar, Jeri, 118
self, yourself, 33–36, 101–24, 183–84, 187–88
   aging and, 112–14, 117, 122, 126, 128, 132, 136, 167
   assertion of, 109–11
   change and, 34–36, 115
   crises and, 101–3, 105, 123
   Fertile Void and, 15
   finances and, 105, 109–10, 112–13, 115–16, 118–23
   future needs and, 114–15, 118, 120–22
   neglect of, 107
   prioritizing for, 108–9, 112
   responsibilities and, 108, 123–24
   rest of your life and, 164–67, 169, 176, 179
   saying no and, 60
   support systems for, 116–18, 122
   taking care of, 104–24, 126, 164–67, 169, 188
selfishness, 48, 78, 186
   and care of self, 104, 112–13, 124
Senility Prayer, 130–31
Serenity Prayer, 129–30
sex, sexuality, 66, 143, 172–73
   aging and, 3, 126, 130–31, 136–41
   renegotiating marriages and, 145, 147, 151–53
   rest of your life and, 173, 176
   in well-being, 136–39
Shulman, Alix Kates, 87–88
Shut up and Live! (Downs), 143
siblings, 146, 168
   crises and, 94, 96–98
   friendships and, 64, 73
   new normal and, 91–92
   saying no and, 58–59
Simon, Carly, 91
Social Security, 8, 177

society, 14, 89, 105, 143
  aging and, 3, 8, 21
  change and, 23, 28
  friendships and, 65, 70, 78
  gender discrimination and, 5
  rest of your life and, 164, 173
  saying no and, 54–55, 58, 60
solitude, 35, 40, 81
"Song to Sensuality" (Angelou), 131–32
speaking up:
  change and, 33–34
  renegotiating marriages and, 152, 156–57
  saying no and, 42, 45–49, 53, 55, 62, 152
Speier, Jackie, 122–23
spirituality, 26, 127, 183, 186
  renegotiating marriages and, 151–52
spouses, 5–7
  aging and, 6–7, 12
  and care of self, 107–9, 112, 115, 122–23, 166
  change and, 37–38
  crises and, 85–87, 92, 95, 98, 101
  friendships and, 64, 70–71, 76, 80–81
  rest of your life and, 162, 166–67, 172–73
  saying no and, 43–44, 46, 59–60, 152
  see also marriage
Steinem, Gloria, 3, 71
stress, 82, 163
  aging of body and, 135–36
  friendships and, 79–80, 84
  renegotiating marriages and, 154–55
  saying no and, 51–52, 59–60

Taylor, Shelley E., 79–81
testosterone, 25, 52–53, 137, 158
This Is Not the Life I Ordered (Stephens, Speier, Risley, and Yanehiro), 81, 102–3, 107, 122–23
Thomas, Marlo, 28–29
time, 57, 182
  aging of body and, 128
  and care of self, 113–14, 117
  crises and, 103
  in Fertile Void, 15–17
  friendships and, 63, 84
  renegotiating marriages and, 146, 149
To Love What Is (Shulman), 88
Too Soon Old, Too Late Smart (Livingston), 27

Transition Network, The (TTN), 56, 116–17
travel, 17, 52, 187
  change and, 23, 26, 32, 35, 37
  friendships and, 66–67
  new normal and, 100
  renegotiating marriages and, 146, 150–52, 155–57
  rest of your life and, 161–62, 173
trust, 112
  friendships and, 65–66, 70–72, 74–76, 81
  renegotiating marriages and, 146–47, 153

Uncharted Territory (Rubin), 112
"Upstaging Time" (Paley), 10

Vaillant, George E., 143, 145, 169
Van Allen, Karen, 69
volunteerism, 70, 86
  and care of self, 109–10
  change and, 35–36
  rest of your life and, 163, 172

weight changes, 26, 34, 71
  aging of body and, 125, 130
  rest of your life and, 160, 169–70
Weil, Andrew, 129, 169
West, Mae, 164
White House Project, 110
widows, widowers, 97, 116, 140, 175
wisdom, 101, 183, 185
WomanSage, 178
women:
  femininity of, 145
  feminism of, 5, 56
  legacy of limitations on, 12–14
  statistics on, 14, 54, 74–75, 119, 122
  uniqueness of, 9, 11–12
Women's Campaign Forum (WCF), 110
World According to Garp, The (Irving), 90

yes, saying, 45, 51, 56, 58–62
Young, Laurie, 119
Young, Valerie, 165
yourself, *see* self, yourself
youth, 2–4, 14, 69
  as ideal state, 2–3, 52
  rest of your life and, 171–72